Major planting
Netting:
, Line & Spearfishing
Major planting
Kumaras, etc
BARREN
TIREA
OLATA
OUE-NUKU
OKORO or MAWETE
TAMATEA KAI-ARIKI
TAMATEA WANANGA
TAMATEA AIO.
TAMATEA WHAKAPAO
HUNA.
ARI-ROA
HOTU
MAWHARU
ATUA WHAKA HAE HAE
OHUA
3
4
5
6
7
8
9
10
11
12
13
14
15
Netting Mullet.
BARREN
Major planting:-
Kumaras, etc.
BARREN
se days.
crops.
Good for crops above
ground level:-
water-mellons.
etc.
CW00969252

DR HINEMOA ELDER

WAWATA

Moon Dreaming

Daily wisdom guided by Hina,
the Māori moon

He kupu whakamihi ki a Hina

Ko te hara a Rona te pūtake e mōhiotia whānuitia ana, kua whakapepehatia hoki te whakataukī nei, 'Kia mahara ki te hē a Rona'.

Tērā tētahi wahine kō Rona tōna ingoa, nō tētahi pō ka tonoa ia ki te tiki wai. Ko te marama i te pō e tūrama ana i te ara haere ki te pūkaki. Ka tae atu a Rona ki te awa e āta rere atu rā te tūpou e hiahiatia ana. Ka kohia e ia te tūpou ki tāna tahā. Kātahi ka puta mai tētahi kapua ki te rangi. I taua wā, ka ngaro te atarau o te marama, tā te mea kua kapia tōna kanohi e te kapua. Taro rawa ake ka tāpepa a Rona, ā, ka whātorotoro ia i tōna ringa ki tētahi rākau ngaio e tātata ana ki a ia, kia whakamatua ai tōna tū. Ka pā mai te rikarika ki a ia, kia huri atu ia ki te marama, ka kangaia, ka whakaparahakotia.

Ko Hina tētahi ingoa o mua mō te marama.

I te mea i kangaia ia e Rona, ka tīkina atu a Rona e Hina ki te rohe o te whānau mārama. Horekau a Rona i wewete i taua rākau ngaio, i te tahā rānei, ka mauria tonutia e Rona tāna tahā, me te rākau hoki ki te marama. Tae noa ki tēnei wā, e noho tonu ana a Rona ki tō Hina whare.

Ki te āta titiro atu koe ki te marama i te pō, inā he Ōturu, he Rākaunui rānei taua pō, ka kite koe i a Rona e puritia tonutia ana ki te rākau ngaio, he tahā hoki kei tōna uma.

Ka hoki anō ki te whakataukī mō Rona, 'Kia mahara ki te hē a Rona'. He whakaaro nui kei roto i ēnei kupu tuku iho. Kua roa ahau e kōmanawa ana ki aua whakaaro nui, me te kura huna e whakahuahuatia ana e taua whakataukī. Ki a au e rua ngā tū whakamāramatanga o te whakataukī nei, he whakaaraara tētahi, he whakatikatika tētahi. E mea ana ngā kaumātua, ina kitea e koe tētahi hē, whakatikatikangia, ki te kore kei rite koe ki taua hē. Ki a au, he momo manaaki hoki te mahi whakatikatika. Ko te hoa haere o te manaaki ko te aroha.

Tae noa ki tēnei wā e manaakitia ana a Rona e Hina. Ko te mea nui kia ora tonu ngā kōrero tuku iho mō Hina, mō Rona, me tā Hina kaha, pō te ao, ao te pō.

He atua hoki a Hina, he mana anō tōna, he tapu anō tōna. Kei a Hina te mana ki te kukume i ngā tai o Tangaroa me ngā tai hoki o Hinemoana, otirā Te Tai Tamawahine me Te Tai Tamatāne.

Hoi anō, i tōna maeatanga ake kia mahara hoki ki te aroha o Hina ki a tātou e whakaaro ana ki te hē a Rona.

Dedication to Hina

Rona's wrongdoing, the basis of which is widely known, is contained in this whakataukī, this aphorism: 'Let's recall Rona's mistake.'

There was once a woman, Rona was her name. One night she went to fetch water, the moon lighting her path. Rona arrived beside the stream, where the water that she needed was flowing peacefully by. She collected the water in her gourd. At that very moment, a cloud passed across the sky. The moon's light was abruptly obscured, the face hidden from view. In the dark, Rona tripped and reached out her hand to a nearby ngaio tree in order to steady herself. In her anger she turned swiftly, railing at the moon.

Hina is an old name for the moon.

Because Rona swore at her, Hina took Rona up to her celestial home. Rona didn't let go of the ngaio tree, or her gourd. She persisted in holding onto her gourd, and the tree, while on the moon. Since then and until now, Rona remains in Hina's realm.

If you look carefully at the moon at night, whether at Ōturu or at Rākaunui, you will see Rona, still holding onto the ngaio tree, her gourd close to her chest.

Returning to the proverbial saying, ‘Let’s recall Rona’s mistake.’ There is a great deal of wisdom in these words passed down from ancient times. I have long mulled over their acumen, and the lessons from when the saying was coined. To my way of thinking, there are two aspects. One is a warning, and one is about making amends. Our old people say, if one makes a mistake, correct it. For me, manaaki, generosity of spirit, is present within the process of correcting mistakes. The partner of this manaaki is empathy.

From that time to this, Hina provides Rona with manaaki. A central theme kept alive in this account of old about Hina, about Rona, is Hina’s fortitude throughout both night and day.

Hina is also a goddess. As well as her shining attributes, she has other powers and influence, other sacred roles. It is Hina who draws the tides of the oceans, the tides of the east coast and of the west coast, the tides of human beings.

And so, Hina’s compassion is revealed when we remember Rona’s mistake.

Contents

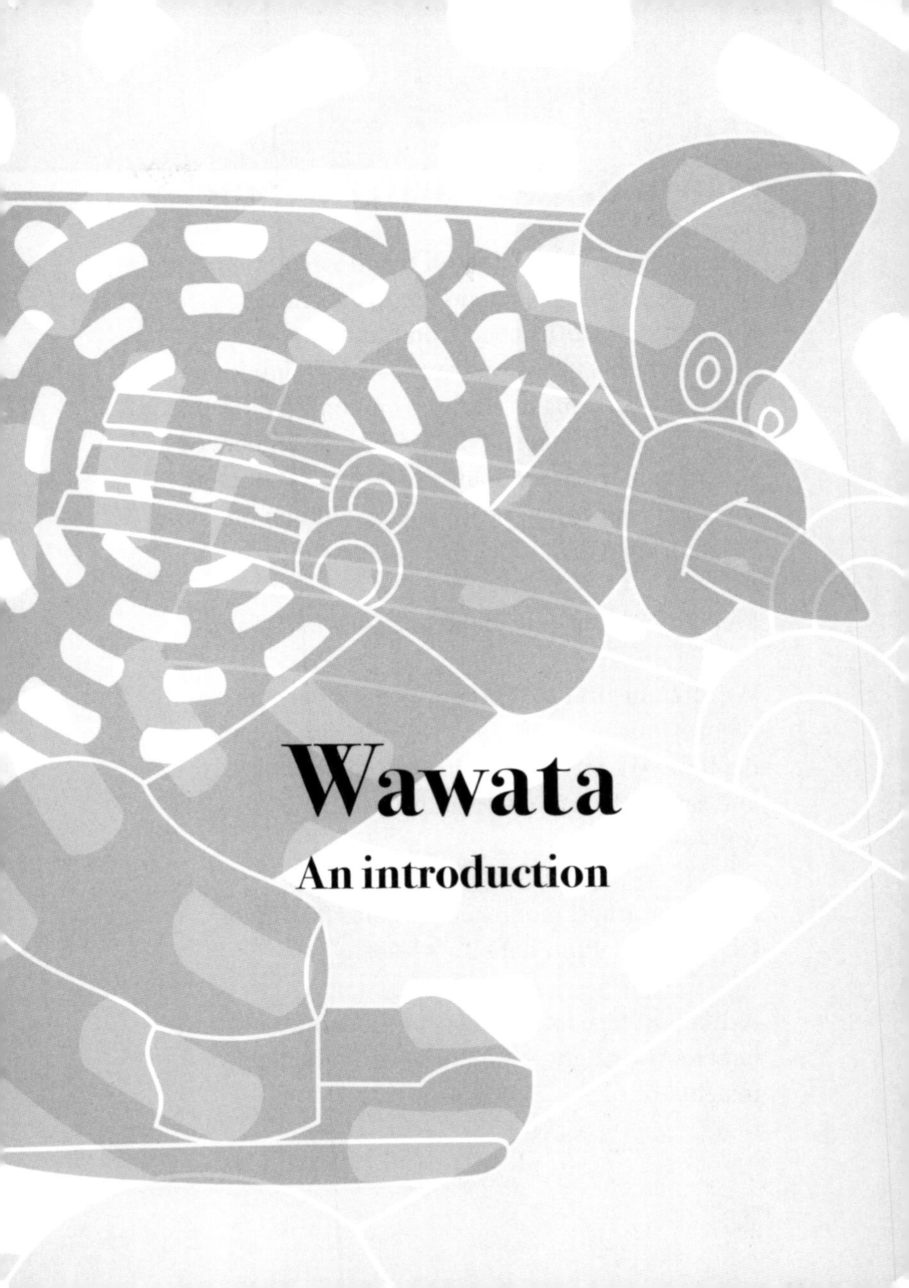

Wawata

An introduction

Nau mai, haere mai, welcome.

Telling stories by the light of the moon is something I picture our old people doing. Adventurous escapades of our forebears unfolding to open the door for our wawata, our own dreams. Thinking about the retelling of stories by moonlight has that magical quality, doesn't it? Around the embers of that imaginary fire. Looking up at the sky, feeling that eerie, cool and ever-changing light on our skin. Inviting us to drift off as our dreams take over.

Moon dreaming — through both day and night.

We often neglect that other precious part of our moon's journey, where she relentlessly traverses our daytime. We forget that our lunar companion rises and sets with us at different times across the day as well as the night.

Hina, our Māori moon goddess, has 30 different faces to help illuminate life's lessons.

A different face for each day of the month. And with her changing light, new stories are revealed. New insights.

This is a book of stories for us, seen through Hina's luminescent gaze. Each day's face with its own precious name. Our old people reach forward into our lives, with each of our moon's names as their offerings, as their reminders — a chance for us to connect to that ancient wisdom, their ancient technology, a source of strength in our strange modern world.

This book is designed to open up our moon dreams, for a deeper, more affectionate and more intimate connection with ourselves and others.

Connection and relationship are the basis of our wellbeing. Only now, with these central experiences of our lives being so highly restricted, do we suddenly feel the impact of that pain and loss at their absence. Only now do we truly appreciate how much we need to feel connected.

The pandemic which rages on in different forms — isolation, social distancing and the interwoven tsunami of death, long-term effects, mental distress, horror and fear — continuing to strike at all of us. The climate emergency of our mother earth, Papatūānuku, evidence of the deepening destruction we have caused our planet, surrounds us. Both of these phenomena, together with wars and displacement, combine to corrode our experiences of health and wellbeing.

As a mother, friend, descendant, lover, ancestor of the future, and as a psychiatrist, I have borne witness to the devastation of the pandemic on our experiences of intimacy.

We have such a profound loss of closeness, of touch, of seeing each other's expressions. Alongside the horrifying deaths across the globe, we have felt such numbing loss, often hard to name or to put into words. We are all in so much emotional pain. Even though we hate to admit it, this mental anguish, this disconnection has changed our world forever.

How do we reclaim the richness of connectivity, a fulfilling experience of intimacy in the context of the ravages of social distancing? Our separation and our loneliness, alongside our fear of proximity? How do we discover ways to open up our innermost sources of resilience to express how much we need to be connected in order to feel well? Deliberately drawing on our ancient indigenous wisdom about this concept we call 'time' opens up this source of wellbeing.

Our tūpuna, our ancestors, had a different relationship with time. They recognised time as part of the natural world's life cycle. And our Moon, Hina, this mysterious female deity, has long held a special role in signalling the different energies of time across each month.

Hina's travels have fascinated me for many years. I recently dug out some of my old maramataka, my Māori calendars, that I kept from the mid 2000s. Hina's influence in my life has taken on more and more potency over the years. Connecting back with our old people's knowledge about her role in nature and therefore her effect on us. Opening up a deeper awareness of our place in the natural world, we begin to feel our insignificance, our place in the order of things. Not an easy path. Fraught and sad, lonely and frustrating at times. Lessons we thought we had learned come back around with each month's cycle and remind us of deeper layers and blind spots. And when we do find a growing sense of place, of harmony, there is such a sense of release. A new kind of freedom starts to emerge.

Our most 'feeling' selves if you like. This is the journey where our minds can wander, where we can begin to dream. Hina provides a natural resetting while we travel with her across the month. She guides us with the qualities of each luminous reflection, soothing our modern-day pain and suffering.

For us, each day of the Māori lunar rotation has its own special name. Thirty different names.

It felt like a lot to get my head around to start with. So to be honest, one of the reasons I started writing this book was because I was trying to find ways to remember each of the faces Hina shows us through the month.

I needed Hina's stories to help me. And I needed to discover the stories her different guises awoke in me.

This is the book I wish I had read when I was young.

I wish I had known time through Hina's movements. I wish I had known the names of our moon's face around her cycle every month. I wish I had that deeper awareness and anticipation of her influence from the centre of who I am, knowing that intrinsic lunar connection to all of the life around me. Connected to earth, sea and sky. To planting gardens, harvesting and fishing. To the tides of what it means to be human.

I wish I had known that our ancestors' wisdom was there for me every single day. I wish I had that wisdom with me to reflect on their meanings for all of us, for my loved ones, every day of every month. Hina's guidance through each day as I passed through my life as a descendant, a sister, a mother, a partner, a doctor. I wish I had been immersed in our Māori understandings of her luminescence for all that time.

My heart mourns that loss so deeply. I wonder what that would be like, to grow up in a world where all of that depth of awareness is simply part of our lives. Part and parcel of ordinary daily life. I have daydreams, wawata, about that. Over the years I have kept these maramataka, my Māori calendar diaries, noting down my thoughts each day. As I return to these I smile. It feels like tūpuna are drawing me back, beckoning me and spurring me on. Since then I have felt compelled to read as much as I could from others. To listen and learn about Hina's travels and the lessons embedded in them.

As these stories began to flow, I realised that Hina's month-long journey has phrases, just like refrains in a song. And yes, I mean phrases, not only phases which we usually associate with our moon. Each night joining the melodic flow from what has preceded it and melting into the next. The energy builds and subsides just like a series of lines from a tune stuck in your head, surging to formidable crescendo peaks, then descending into periods of lilting final notes, hanging in the air, drifting away into a final quiet pause. A place to draw breath.

Hina's musical phrases suddenly took charge of me. The six central clusters of Hina's manifestations revealing themselves as akin to the progression through the different styles of our waiata and haka that are so awe-inspiring at Te Matatini, the biennial national competition of Māori performing arts. This year marks 50 years of Te Matatini. As your moon dreaming wawata lead you through Hina's musical energies, you will feel the profound influence Te Matatini can have on our daily lives.

The first group of nights form our whakaeke, our entrance. From the darkness of Whiro, the light door of our lunar cycle opens. Then our laments, our mōteatea of the Tamatea moons are next. The waiata ā-ringa, the action songs, follow on with their movements, elegant and beguiling. Taking us through to the twin orbs, our poi, Rākaunui and Rākaumatohi. Five days with compelling haka rhythms come next.

And lastly, whakawātea, clearing the way, the final act of closure. A series of salutes to the deities Tangaroa, Tāne and Rongo, to our priorities in Maurea and finally Mutuwhenua. Experiencing time, shaped by Hina's changing harmonies.

And so this book started to come to life.

The power of travelling with our moon, through every day and night of the month, has freed up Hinengaro, goddess of the mind, and released an intimate sense of being alive. From the pitch blackness in Whiro to the revealing spotlight of Rākaunui and around to Whiro again.

A kind of mirimiri, a traditional Māori massage technique. Gradually easing the knots of pent-up tension in mind and body — some old intergenerational tangles and scars.

Each of Hina's faces, each of her journeys across

Ranginui, our sky father, providing a distinctive vantage point for comfort, and for challenge to our stagnant, complacent ways. Each change in her appearance, a tender glimpse revealing new insights into our need for connection. A safe, daily journey to reflect on our passions and desires, our vulnerabilities, facing fear of rejection and abandonment, our jealousy, our shame, guilt and loss. Somehow our moon's trajectory across the sky in various guises of light and shadow is an invitation to talk about deep-seated emotions. About things which sometimes we might prefer to keep hidden. And in this era of such restriction and social isolation, the need to rediscover sexual feelings and sexuality, sensuality, touch. Our interwoven emotional and physical needs.

Every month of our lives. The incremental opening and closing of our moon's aperture, a mirror of our own lives' cycles, birth and death. How the circle returns to itself. These ever-present truths await us. Every single day. Our growth, our spurts of energy and our development, all watched over by Hina, high above us. Times to return to rest and to gather together. Times for silent soul searching. Times for joy. These are the stories I have discovered. Hina has unleashed these moon-dreaming stories.

In some dreams we defy the laws of physics. We can fly. Sometimes we can't move and no matter how much we scream, no sounds come from our mouths. In some we can breathe under water. Our dreams can give us special powers, like talking with animals. In some we experience fantasies that seem way outside our real-life preferences. Sometimes our dreams carry our worries and fears; our most delicate and vulnerable aspects can be unmasked in dreams too. Our dreams wake us sometimes, shocked, maybe ashamed and struggling to tell the difference between our dreams and reality.

This is a book for us to dream by. A book to weave stories by the light of the Māori moon, month after month after month. A cycle where we can revisit our energies, our themes, our scary places every month. A practice where we honour each of Hina's faces in all her glory, and see ourselves and our need for connection in her mirror.

This is at the heart of Hina's message. There is flow in life, shifting awareness, sometimes with almost imperceptible changes, our processing happening over a series of nights. I began witnessing these waves of time as the lunar tides drew me deeper into a female sense of knowing. Stories from the deep storehouse of our whare tangata, stories from the womb.

Following Hina's travels has encouraged me to share some stories of my journey as a woman. The need to pass on these stories became so strong, fuelled by my observation of the loss of transmission of our female stories for generations to come. Hina's influence has drawn me closer to some of our female forebears and goddesses, made me mull over their lessons and their wisdom as they wax and wane their moonlight into our own lives and those of the future generations.

I have focused on female energy and stories, and at the same time, I welcome readers from all genders, however people identify. We are all born from a mother. Learning more about Hina's cycle, our lunar calendar's hidden gifts, opens up new insight and enlightenment for everyone.

A number of iwi have different names for some of the days and nights of the month. The names I have used and the flow they speak to has become most meaningful to me from our Okoro, completed by my whanaunga Ted Jones. These are not the only names nor the only ways to feel the energies of each day. And some iwi begin the lunar cycle with Rākaunui. What is so exciting is that there are now a growing number of resources to support our knowledge about Hina and our Māori lunar calendar. Together, these support our ongoing efforts to bring our ancestors' wisdom into daily life, for the better, strengthening our wellbeing.

I have written the body of each day's story on that particular day. I wanted to truly surrender to Hina's specific influence as the source of inspiration for each of the stories.

Ko ngā wawata a Hina.

Dreaming under Hina's influence.

This book of Hina's invitations to dream has been road-tested too, by a small ope, a band of my loved ones, helping to check in with how a wider audience might receive these pūrākau, these stories.

I must admit to my own struggles with using maramataka in book form. A start and finish can give the appearance that time stretches away in a straight line, only forwards and backwards. Months following on from each other in a stepwise fashion with each page of the diary. Each month further and further away, until the end of the book, the end of the year. Each moon's lessons recorded separately. I looked for ways to return to that same moon each month to collect my experiences at that time of Hina's journey. I felt the need to circle back and collect deeper understandings for each of Hina's 30 lessons. This aspect is an inherent tension in presenting time in a book form. So with this book I invite you to keep returning to the beginning, month after month, and consider how each of Hina's faces frees up wawata for you. And to build your own storehouse of wawata stories. Over and over again. I have made sure that there is room to make your own notes in the margins.

Making dreams come true starts with the dream itself. This book is one way for me to turn my wawata into reality. Bringing forward these personal Hina reflections, adding to the opportunities for our tamariki and mokopuna to grow up with a different experience of time, through Hina's eyes. My hope is that we can all connect to healthier futures for generations to come through different wawata, under Hina's guidance.

'Nā Hina te pō, nā Hina te ao'. Both darkness and light belong to Hina.

This whakataukī from back home in Te Rarawa, in the Far North, reminds us of Hina's power. Let the book usher the Māori moon in all her glory and intrigue into your life. Travel through each day and night with our moon goddess beside you. Feel what that changes in your experience of time. What time through Hina's lens is trying to reveal to you, about you and yours. Make time for dreaming. Whatever the time of day. Relish the freedom that dreaming opens up.

We all carry stories of leaders in our whānau, in our whakapapa, our lines of descent, that lend themselves to different nights of the month. These stories can bring you into their close embrace. And a reminder, that you are representatives of those ancestors, living now.

Maybe it is time for you to begin to live their dreams. The dreams they had about you. And to draw on the wisdom and lessons for connection and intimacy with Hina's watchful eye on your dreams throughout each precious day.

1
Whakaeke

Ki ngā whakaeke, haumi.

Join with those who connect the waka together.

Find your place, you are part of the action.

Our entrance onto Hina's moon stage begins our lunar journey. This is our whakaeke.

The prefix 'whaka-' always indicates action, movement, causation. And the word 'eke' is a verb with a lot of energy concentrated inside this dynamic triad of letters. It has a real onomatopoeia. 'Eke' is a word with oomph to its signature. It means to come in to land, to get on board, to embark, to ascend. The word itself really makes an entrance.

Whiro, Tirea, Ohata, Ōuenuku, Okoro. Our entrance into Hina's realm is vital. This is how we set ourselves up to dream of connection and a more open and intimate experience of living.

The next five moons are our fundamentals, our tūāpapa, our baseline. What we stand on. And traversing the next five days and nights helps us to clarify both where we stand and what we stand for. We rebuild ourselves from here each month. Hina provides the opportunity for a fresh start, for a renewed entry every month.

It seems fitting to begin the whakaeke with our precious Okoro, our moon dial from home.

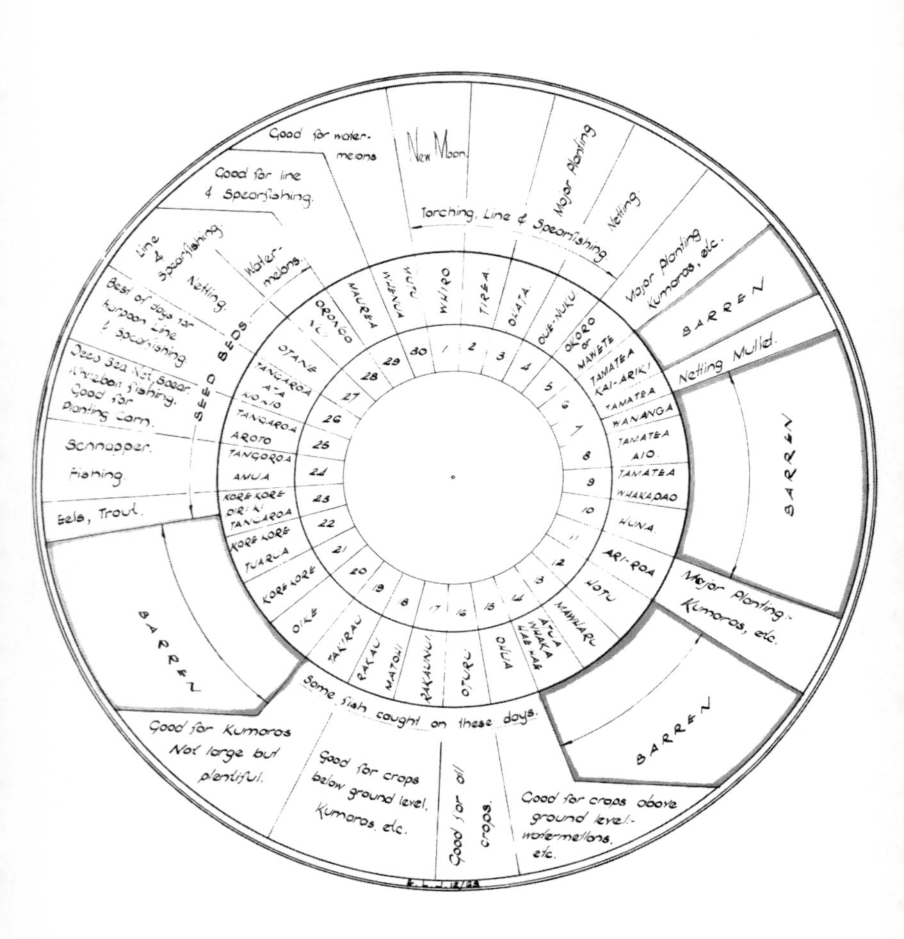
Good for water-melons
New Moon
Major Planting
Good for line & Spearfishing
Torching, Line & Spearfishing
Netting
Line & Spearfishing
Netting
Water-melons
Major Planting Kumoros, etc.
BARREN
Best of days for harpoon Line & Spearfishing
SEED BEDS
Netting Mullet
Deep Sea Net, Spear Whitebait fishing. Good for Planting Corn
BARREN
Schnapper Fishing
Eels, Trout
Major Planting:- Kumoros, etc.
BARREN
BARREN
Some fish caught on these days.
Good for Kumoros Not large but plentiful.
Good for crops below ground level, Kumoros, etc.
Good for all crops.
Good for crops above ground level:- watermellons, etc.

I first saw this taonga, this treasure, hanging on the wall in my cousin Peter-Lucas Jones' house in Taipā in 2020. It stopped me in my tracks. I could not believe my eyes. I had been slowly working on this book for more than a year already, drawing stories together and going back over my old maramataka, my moon calendars. In that instant I recognised a familar circular language. This way of depicting Hina's travels reminded me of the concentric wheels of our whakapapa, our genealogy, drawn by our mum's father, Tommy Bowman.

This orbital language spoke to me in a way I recognised so well.

Ted (Edward) Llewellyn Jones, our whanaunga, our relation, made this Okoro in 1969.

And yes, Okoro is the name of one of the days and nights of this lunar calendar too. At that time, Ted had just left Kaitāia College. He was 16 years old and living with his grandmother, Raiha Moeroa Jones, Mā Jones as she was known, who still lived in the house where she had had many of her 16 tamariki.

Ted told me how Mā Jones and Tā Hekenukumai Busby, our illustrious navigator, asked Ted to meet them. He recounted how they passed him bits of paper and told him to put them together to make this lunar calendar, this Okoro. As Ted put it, he 'hopped on the drawing board'. And this is what he made.

Tā Hek had the idea of the circle. The circular nature of time unmistakable. And so our revolving taonga came to life, the numbers designed to rotate, the continuity of lunar time enshrined for generations to come.

Ted has graciously allowed the taonga to be represented in this book. Another way for our mātauranga, our traditional Māori wisdom, to be humbly shared. Our ancestor's legacy lives on. Seeing this beautiful moon dial was such a tohu, a wonderful and telling portent. A sign for me to continue, to follow through and complete these stories.

Our whakaeke phase is about entering. It is the word used to describe the walk towards the wharenui, the meeting house, from the waharoa or gateway. And it is the name of the performance of the items that bring our kapa, our group, onto the stage. In this way, it is like many such words, functioning as both a verb and noun.

The whakaeke is our portal onto Hina's stage. Whiro, then Tirea, Ohata and then Ōuenuku and Okoro illuminate our foundations, our origins, our truths. And we are not alone.

We enter with our friends, our relations, even when we are physically apart, we can call on them to be part of our whakaeke. And of course we bring those who have passed on with us too. Our tūpuna who instigated the Okoro, Mā Jones, Tā Hek, our Karani Pāpā, Tommy, and many many others. We travel in convoy, already aligned with so many.

Here we go. Freeing up our wawata, our dreams, for the start of our round trip with Hina.

Whiro

Renewal

Kia katia ō karu kia pai ai te kite.

Close your eyes in order to truly perceive.

Let the darkness of Whiro open your eyes.

Whiro is where we begin our lunar journey.

Whiro is our name for the new moon. The darkness. A brief re-enactment of Te Pō. Our long night of creation. Our moon's lustre completely obscured. Her face illuminated away from our gaze, on the other side. The side we never see.

Whiro signals beginnings and endings. Birth and death. Spring tide. The great washing away. A giant reset.

Here in the dark. Breathing in the darkness, my chest rising and falling with Whiro. Inhalations adding to the space deep inside, deep enough to be completely immersed in that luscious centre of my feminine being. Exhalations allow the release of old patterns. Stepping gently out of those old skins into freshly formed layers of realisation. Confidence starting to grow from that central hidden core of our being.

Welcome to this, our ancient Māori lunar cycle. Whiro welcomes us into her jet-black stare. She is in a class of her own. Her legacy is unique. Her wawata, her dreams, take us beyond our obsidian-hard walls of fear into what might be possible.

Whiro-te-tipua is one of the children of Papatūānuku, our earth mother and Ranginui, our sky father. Whiro is sometimes associated with the dark side of humanity. And yet our Whiro moon is so much more than that.

For me Whiro's gift is so eloquently summed up by our tūpuna, our forebears, in the phrase 'Ngā Ika a Whiro'. Literally, Whiro's army. The name for a group of experienced warriors.*

---

* Ika can also mean fish, and victim, but not in this context.

I love that name, it is a name I belong to. A name that claims me back.

It is the name also given to graduates of Te Pīnakitanga o Te Reo Kairangi, a total immersion te reo Māori language course at Te Wānanga o Aotearoa. Forever language warriors, tongues forged in the fire of Whiro. The quest and the responsibility of speaking up for our reo, our language, at all times and in all places is upon us. Discovery of inner purpose and drive is the essence of Whiro for me. This experience was an ultimate shedding of language skin. Right in te muramura o te ahi, the heat of the battle, the fierce flames of learning our language, like a brand on my heart. This experience changed me forever. For the better.

It added potency to the threads binding me to my true identity as Māori. Looking into Whiro's dark eye, into infinite space, somehow manifests those ancient dreams, flying through space and time. Time guided by Whiro. A time of the ongoing learning battle within myself, the battles against whakamā, fear and shame, feelings of inadequacy, the pain of learning and failing and getting up again to keep trying. Battle-scarred and weary at times, yet still here, standing firm. Replenished for another month in Whiro.

We are all warriors of one kind or another. We all have our battles with our own special kind of pain. So it's that time again. A time to rebirth our warrior selves in Whiro.

This Whiro darkness makes our other senses more acute. I hear the ruru, our owl, hunting. That haunting call ringing out through the valley. That portent of those from beyond the ārai, beyond the veil. They are so close tonight and I think of Turikātuku, one of my tūpuna wāhine, my female ancestors. She holds my face tonight in Whiro.

Turikātuku knew about darkness. She gradually went blind, it is said, from some kind of inflammatory disease. Despite her blindness, she was a warrior, she fought in battle, she was a military strategist and she was a matakite, a seer. A true wahine toa, a warrior woman. Turikātuku was born in the late 1700s and married the Ngāpuhi chief Hongi Hika.

It is said she spoke these words about her descendants buried in Australia, whose remains were not returned as she had wished, 'Ka tohe au, ka tohe au'. I will persevere, I will persevere.

This is my whisper to myself. To persevere, no matter my inability to see in the dark. To find my way carefully at this time of the month. For me the dark mantle of Whiro is a protective time for insights, a time to call on that deep core of resistance and fight for what is right.

So we begin again in the time of Whiro, our new moon. Te tai nunui, the first syzygy. What a word! The name for the alignment of our moon and sun's gravitational forces. Pulling the oceans high and drawing them fiercely back again. The first spring tide. The combined forces of Tamanuiterā, our sun, and Whiro. A chance to renew from a deep inner place of truth.

A chance to dream ourselves into the vastness of space.

How will you renew yourself in this dark moon's infinite energy tonight? What stories can you draw on from your old people, from women in your extended family, to replenish your strength for Hina's new orbit? Isn't it strange how being in the dark can make what matters clear? Now, close your eyes and see.

Tirea

New learnings

Kua tuwhera te tomokanga a Hina.

Hina's door is open.

We start with the fundamentals.

Tirea is, for me, the first light. Hina's moon door ever so slightly ajar.

Tirea follows Whiro, the so called 'new moon'.

The first voice. This first burst of energy after Whiro's darkness. The chink of light.

That inescapable invitation, opening us up again after being completely enveloped in the calming moon shadow. Hina's tiny hint of a smile. Kuhu mai. Come in.

Tirea signals the beginning of the flow of four

days that are a fitting time for building new learnings and reflections. To set the scene for the coming month. It is the right time to reflect on our decisions and our compromises. The fundamentals. And how we communicate these stories to ourselves and to others. To build connection both inside and out. This is the deep undercurrent that strengthens our wellbeing across the month.

Today we begin to tap into that invitation to open ourselves up.

Somehow this first glimmer of light has such intensity. Even though Hina only reveals just a fraction of her surface, we sense her vast curvature. We sense huge possibilities, our own histories, our raw truths, coming into the light. She cuts straight to the chase. Tirea's penetrating gaze directs us to start with our basics. Some of those lessons right at the core of our being. These fingers of light beckon us to begin our lunar ride up this first wave of our moon's rising energy.

My intuition, deep in my puku, in my gut, connects with this tiny opening of our moon's door. We can speak about how decisions and compromises have shaped our lives.

It suprises me how those moments in life, times that have felt neatly packed away, undisturbed in the attic of the mind, can suddenly take on a fresh meaning. They demand to be reconsidered. Turns out this spring-clean at the spring tide can be a rugged old journey back through some parts of my life that were still pretty sore.

It is a sad reality that most of us have experienced more than one situation where our freedom, our choices have been violated in some way. I was taken aback by the detail of memories that flew through that sliver of Tirea's light, as soon as I started on this mind-path.

I remember that contraception was once one difficult area to navigate. When I was younger I did not feel I could always assert myself in this critical part of safe and healthy sexual connection. I look back on that now and see how little confidence I had in communicating these essentials. I was assessing how much value my perspectives, my rights, my body meant in those exchanges. And I discovered it meant very little. What I realise now is how little I thought of myself. How little I felt my body was worth. I am shocked when I think back. Why was I, a well educated and, to all intents and purposes, a strong confident woman, so afraid to assert myself in the bedroom? I was afraid of rejection, humiliation, of being judged, being labelled. Easier for me at that time to compromise myself, the potential price felt too high to pay.

Asking for what we need sexually, is that a clear decision, and how often do we compromise? How safe do we feel communicating what feels good and doesn't feel good? And in what we share, what we offer, what we choose to share sexually with our partners, how much of a decision or compromise is that?

Even keeping the light on or having the light off was a dilemma. I remember being so shy to have the light on when I was young. Shy that I would be criticised, that my body would be found inadequate. Now I wonder why I wasted time and energy on such concerns. But that was my headspace back then. And I see those same fears about body shaming haven't gone away with our next generations. The scrutiny and value placed on certain kinds of bodies remains a cornerstone of our societies. How can we shift these draconian views and judgmental practices about our bodies? How to fully embrace acceptance of the fluidity of body types and genders? How and what we decide and why we compromise reflects our values and our priorities. It communicates who we are.

By this glowing light of Tirea, I wonder how we can undress our thoughts about who we are, according to the lessons embedded in our decisions and compromises.

Hina's first tiny taste of radiance invites us to stand in our own growing sense of self-determination. To be kind about past decisions and how we might choose differently now.

How could you take some time today to reflect on understanding earlier choices and what they teach us about the future, should similar situations occur again? What are our forgiving wawata, our dreams that find forgiveness for ourselves? Take your loving pillow-talk dreams to bed tonight.

Ohata

Celebrate menstrual flow

Mai i Kurawaka.

From the red earth of Kurawaka.

Where we are from is who we are.

Ohata, or Ohoata as she is called in some areas, follows Tirea in this first phrase of our moonlit musical journey. Our whakaeke, re-establishing, re-asserting what matters to us.

Ohata is a moon that rises in the middle of the morning and sets before midnight. She travels with us through the day.

I use my own basic literal translation to understand the blending of 'oho' and 'ata'. Oho being to get up, to arise, to awaken, to be roused and ata being morning. Morning awakening. Interestingly 'oho' can also mean productive or fruitful. Our tūpuna, our ancestors, weave their nuances into these words for us to ponder.

This is the part of our month where I reflect on my years with te awa o te atua.

My menstrual cycle, my fertility and the sacredness of this aspect of our lives as wāhine, as women. My awa, my menstrual blood flow, often arriving in the morning.

Our monthly cycle of shedding the lining of the whare tangata, the womb, is such a powerful experience. And yet one that colonisation has steeped in shame. We are still carefully taught this is a 'mate', an illness. Reclaiming our healthy identity as women who experience this ancient aspect of our lineage is an essential element of our wellbeing and our truth.

Our awa, our menstruation, is such a profound and clear link with the natural world, with our environment. With the cycles of life. Whero, red, the colour of blood. Glowing with sacred reverence. The crimson hue of the birds' feathers most highly sought after by our ancestors. Scarlet florets of our coastal guardian pōhutukawa mistaken for such birds by our tūpuna from their waka on the ocean. Whero, synonymous with life, fertility, survival and status.

And yet when colonisers came, such was the power of their brainwashing, that healthy female cycles were deemed dangerous, were thought of as a disease.

The colour of menstrual blood was not shown in advertising of so called 'sanitary' products when I was growing up, either. It was always a blue dye. How confusing. I asked my mum why they didn't show the actual blood. She told me, 'Men make these ads, honey, and they want us to stay ashamed of our bodies.' Knowing this at an intellectual and gut level doesn't necessarily change the insidious impact on how we feel about our bodies functioning. I was so quick to judge my body, my blood. To think of it as dirty. I needed to actively remind myself that this was not true.

My wish is that young women of today and those of the future are free from those oppressive lies. Free from that internalising we have to work hard to unshackle.

Free from our learned self-loathing.

At least now we have some options, moon cups being a brilliant one. Better for the planet too. And it means we get to know our bodies, we get to normalise looking at and touching these cherished parts of who we are. I have had some hilarious times with my daughter after she introduced me to moon cups. Calling out to her in the next room while I struggled in the bathroom with insertion and removal, leaving us in fits of giggles. Perhaps because there were years of nervous energy and conflicted feelings about touching my body to release.

Our tūpuna used resources from their taiao, their environment, during this time of the month.

'Ki te tiki pounamu, ki a Awarua hei kope toto'.*

Prized like the greenstone, so is the awarua padding for blood staunching.

The awarua, 'hygienic absorbent pads used during

---

* *Ngā Mōteatea, The Songs*, A. T. Ngata and P. Te Hurinui Jones, Auckland University Press, 2005, pages 32, 33, 35.

menstruation which were discarded after use'. We witness the practicality of our old people's relationship with Papatūānuku, Earth Mother.

I imagine Kurawaka, Papatūānuku's precious fertile area, the red earth under our Ohata moon. That earth that was used to shape the first human, a woman. Hineahuone, the woman made from earth. Today I celebrate the sacred red flow again. My wawata, my dreams, celebrate our connection to our first woman, to our earth, and to our acceptance of our true selves.

Those who do not experience menstruation are in my wawata too. The fear and embarrassment that might be present for them. How to return to that mutual respect for the sacred aspects of each person's body that was critical for the survival of our ancestors?

How to demystify for those who feel trapped on the outside of the discussion about periods? Those labelled as part of the problem? How to include those who also feel stuck by these labels that pathologise the female body? Imprisoned by those ideas set up by men of another era, of another generation. Talking about our awa, sharing how we feel, accepting help if we are in pain and feeling the need for emotional support. This opens up and normalises our experiences. And for those that don't experience this awa for whatever reason, Ohata is a day to focus on education and self awareness.

Look for Ohata in your sky. How could this time of the month help with new reflections about your 'time of the month', past, present and future? How might you free yourself from any negative thoughts about your awa and celebrate your flow? How can we safely ensure that everyone honours the sacred river on this activating day of Ohata?*

---

* If you want to read more about this kaupapa, Dr Ngāhuia Murphy's *Te Awa Atua: Menstruation in the pre-colonial Māori world*, self-published in 2014, is a definitive text.

Ōuenuku

Different points of view

Uenuku tū wae rua.

A rainbow stands in two places.

Put yourself in others' shoes.

Ōuenuku. Uenuku, our rainbow. This is a day of colours, layers of light, layers of meaning. Uenuku, the deity of rainbows is the face of our Hina moon today.

And there is the 'ō' at the beginning. Why is it there? This 'ō' preceding the word means this is a day belonging to Uenuku.

This 'ō' is a clue about connectivity. This intimate belonging between us and our moon today is of such importance. The grammar of our language reflects our relationships with the natural world in the smallest details.

Indeed, 'ō' is used to indicate the nature of the relationship. 'Ō' is for those relationships within our own generation and those older than us. And for friends, they get the 'ō' ranking too. Our partners when described as 'hoa rangatira', our chiefly friends, are also in the 'ō' category. Significantly for us, wai māori, fresh water, is in the 'ō' camp. Is this a coincidence? Uenuku are only seen when sunlight and rain combine.

Ōuenuku's moon follows on from our awa flow of Ohata. In my mind's eye, I see the red of our awa flowing into the base of the rainbow, with the fan of rainbow colours unfurling up above. Like the light spilling from a prism. This extraordinary light festival that we call a rainbow is such an inspiring sight. It stops us in our tracks. Every, single, time.

I have never met a person who shrugged their shoulders at a rainbow.

Uenuku, this atua, this deity, is an important omen and the subject of many stories for different iwi, tribal groups. A fitting whakataukī to acknowledge someone's mana, their standing, is to say, 'Ko Uenuku tāwhana i te rangi.' Literally, it is Uenuku that curves in the sky, meaning, 'your reputation precedes you'. What a calling card!

This expansion of light, arching upwards from the foundation of red, the sacred colour of life, invites an unfolding of our thoughts and feelings. Our dreams open up like delicate paper fans, their pleats stretching out to mirror Uenuku's curve.

Our wawata take us back in time to Uenuku, a specific taonga, a treasured artefact from Tainui, carved between 1200 and 1500 AD. Uenuku has a distinctive carved appearance unlike any other. There are four spikes at the apex and three gaps, which can represent the seven colours of the rainbow. This taonga was lost in a battle in the late 1700s, only to be rediscovered at Lake Ngāroto many years later. It was a centre piece in the famous *Te Maori* exhibition that travelled to the United States in 1984. Now Uenuku stands at Te Whare Taonga o Te Awamutu, Te Awamutu Museum.

Such was the sacred status of Uenuku, he was traditionally given the young leaves from the first kūmara crop as offerings. He was invoked in incantations before battles. As protector, as caretaker, as inspiration.

I have often wondered why our tūpuna, our ancestors, named this particular face of Hina's monthly cycle after Uenuku? What is it about this advancing flow of the month, as our whakaeke, our entrance, progresses, that we can draw on for our wellbeing?

Another whakataukī, a proverbial saying that gives us a clue to reflect on today is 'Uenuku tū wae rua'. Literally, Uenuku stands in two places. And when you think about it, a rainbow does stand in two places with the arch linking them. This saying can be used in a number of ways: indicating someone coming from two tribal groups, two aspects of a situation, or having a foot in both camps. So for me, the spirit of today's moon invites us to consider alternative viewpoints, to put ourselves in others' shoes, to practise empathy.

Our minds traverse Uenuku's colours, reflecting the layers and nuances of our ideas. Oscillating back and forth across the rainbow. This spectrum reflecting back the emotions we feel when we consider other vantage points. Elements of rain and sun which create this extraordinary light show symbolising the tears and the warmth we experience when we stand in the place of others and feel what they feel. Our own experiences expand when we do this. We shift. I imagine our weight shifting from one foot to the other. We find we are more flexible than we thought. Our own inconsistencies are revealed. This Ōuenuku-inspired movement creates readiness, an agility to move forward with new awareness.

And then, without warning, the extraordinary tohu, this sign, is gone. The very nature of Uenuku is ephemeral. Fleeting, transitory, impermanent.

One of the lessons I take from this day each month, is that our lives are short, and to make the most of this day's insights. The simple joy of observing our thoughts. The sustenance that comes from considering life from a different perspective. That is our dialogue with Ōuenuku today.

How can you dream with your mind's rainbow today? Surrender to the journey across your internal rainbow of colours. Resist the urge to settle in one place or the other. There is always another perspective. Feel that impetus to stand in the shoes of others and see what happens.

Okoro

Reflect on connection

Tū ana tātou ki ō tātou pae maunga.

Let us stand on our mountain ranges.

Our tūpuna give us the horizon.

Our wawata, our dreams, bring us back to earth. Today we descend from the rainbow of Ōuenuku and touch our mountains. The cloud piercers. Our mountains are our ancestors, and our ancestral maunga are living, sentient beings. Their peaks the places that embody our hopes and dreams. The places we describe in our pepeha. Pepeha being our introductions about who we are according to these landmarks, these places and their stories and how they connect us. Our mountains stand trusty, resolute, unwavering.

At the end of this first wave, our whakaeke, Hina brings us to these resting places, nestled with our own maunga tūpuna, ancestral mountain dreams.

I have stood at the place where our old people left Rarotonga. The place where the many ocean-going waka, *Kurahaupō*, *Tākitimu*, *Te Arawa*, *Aotea*, *Tokomaru*, *Tainui* and more left for Aotearoa. It is a curious sensation. Feeling my bones start to hum. Their ancient memory sensing their connections in that place. This ancestral blood seeking to be joined with its origins. Hairs rising on the back of my neck, time slowing and stopping. Tears welling up from my puku, from my gut. Standing on that maunga. Remembering that all our islands are mountains rising up out of the ocean. I see our tūpuna pulling islands up out of the water. Dreaming the maunga into reality. Following the paths of the whales, the birds, the clouds and the currents. Guided by their intimate knowledge of the moon and stars, to these islands we call Aotearoa. On this Okoro moon.

The vista, the perspective, the freedom to dream. There is a dizzy intoxication, a rarified air, being at the top of our maunga. And Hinengaro, goddess of the mind, can fly my wawata, my dreams to the mountain peaks, at any time. Especially today.

Okoro is generous with energy for the mountain

climb. Energy from deep in those resonating bones. I can call on that Okoro energy for the climb up those rocky slopes of whatever this day holds. I can draw upon the determination of my ancestors and their wawata. I think about how they must have had to adapt. From the islands of Te Moananui a Kiwa, the vast Pacific Ocean. The terrain and stories of maunga in Aotearoa are unique. The temperature so much colder, with snow and ice. So many new birds and plants.

I am reminded of a story of one of our famous wāhine from Te Hiku o te Ika, the tail of the fish, the Far North. Whangatauatia was her name. She covered the body of her dead relation, Te Kākā, to protect him when he died during a battle. Her husband Pōroa, in seeing his wife's selfless courage, ended the battle. He named the nearby mountain after her to immortalise the brave actions of his wife.

In my dreams I look down from the summit of Whangatauatia. From this height we can see the tuna pools, the home of the eels. Their sinuous slippery bodies dancing to their own rhythm in the depths of the puna, the pool. These were a familar sight to our ancestors from the Pacific.

A well known and well respected feast. As I stand atop our maunga, I feel the water coursing down the mountainsides, replenishing the pools where the tuna swim and feed. The water that caresses the mountainsides is the same water that caresses the tuna. The mountain, the eel, water and the ocean are all connected. The ocean is where they travel to spawn, just once in their lives. Tuna and their puna. An erotic synergy to daydream about today too. I wonder if our tūpuna thought of them in this way. Okoro is also a good night for tuna to be caught and eaten.

Make Okoro a time to reflect on where you stand in all your exquisite connectedness.

Where are your ancestral mountains that wait patiently to hold you up? Or to cloak you with their soft protective shadow? Pull the waters of today's journey towards you and move those rivulets closer. Bring those lofty mountains to you. Let their rocky hands hold your feet safe and sound. Now you can see what they have in store for you. They give you a new vantage point. Share their clarity and clean, clear air. And let the thick strong tuna swim deep into the puna of your dreams too. The waters, tears and sweat of your old people mingle with your tears and sweat. You have their strength today. Make the most of Okoro, rising steadfast, solid and reliable all through the day and night.

2
Mōteatea

Te hau marama mate o te Tamatea.

The ill wind of Tamatea.

Prudent planning, confronting negative emotions and learning to be still.

Tamatea moons across four days are a serious chunk of time to dive deep into what I call our mōteatea bracket every month.

Mōteatea are our songs in the form of chants. So compelling in their sombre tone.

Often telling stories of the journeys of our old people, detailing adversaries finally overcome, laments of loves lost, all allegories of the struggles of life. Four whole days and nights with some essential challenges. Grappling with some grunty kaupapa, topics that we all encounter in our lives. Caution is in the air. Our wawata, our dreams, are in preparation mode, doing the groundwork. There are key lessons to refresh over Hina's second stage.

The name Tamatea gives us some clues. Many great navigators and travellers of old were named Tamatea. Many carry this auspicious name today.

In our own Muriwhenua genealogical line we have several: Tamateanui, Tamatearoa, Tamatea-mai-tawhiti in the generations before Muriwhenua herself. And Tamatea-pōkai-whenua, one of her offspring.

I wonder why the moon was named after these ancestors? Or were they named after these moons?

These were the protagonists, the risk-takers who broke the mould. And in order to survive the unexpected aspects of their quests they had to be prepared. They had to think carefully and balance caution, timing and action. They set themselves up for success. They sought expert counsel, they tuned in to the signs from te taiao, the natural world.

So for me this is a time to dream as our trailblazers of former times did. To question beyond the superficial. To look behind our own masks. The modern world encourages us to put on a brave face in order to fit in. Too often we make ourselves smaller, we deliberately take up less room, not the space we actually need. Faking it until you make it certainly has its place. But the down side of doing that exclusively is we can lose ourselves in the thick of all this pretence.

These four days give us a chance to spend some dedicated time planning and observing, equipping ourselves with determination and honesty. We are building on the foundation we laid in the first five days of the month. Reviewing the principles of our life lessons. Critical to any period of adventure we must factor in our ability to genuinely rest and surrender ourselves to some loving. Timing is everything as they say. And our purposeful refocus is now, this drives our readiness for what is to come.

These are the regular challenges of Hina's Tamatea phase.

An old lament sung at Te Rauparaha's funeral in 1853 included the phrase, 'te hau marama mate o te Tamatea'. Literally, the ill winds of the Tamatea moons. Such was the grief, the pain in mourning for their loved one, the extraordinary Te Rauparaha, the personification of defiance and persistence, who took his people from defeat to victory. And the composer of the famous 'Ka Mate' haka.

The Tamatea moons were a painful time of loss. And we can resonate with those big emotions at this time too. Letting the mask drop as we focus our readiness, the pent-up emotions of anger, rage, frustration that we have tried to hide are revealed. Recognising and then letting those feelings drift away with the winds of Tamatea is such a huge release.

See what the faces of the Tamatea moons have in store for you this month.

The order of these Tamatea moons varies across different iwi, different tribes, as well as the number of Tamatea moons. I have been guided by my whanaunga, my relatives, and the oversight of our esteemed elders.

Let Hina's mōteatea, her chants be your guide. Check your heart and your puku, your gut, for their input. Place your hands there. What do the unforgettable Tamatea dreams reveal for your planning this month?

Tamatea kai-ariki

Be wary of destructive energies

Ko te riri tāne he ahi rarauhe, ko te riri wahine he riri hūngeingei.

Male anger happens in a flash, women's is a slow burn.

Letting anger stew makes us ill.

Tamatea kai-ariki, the first of our Tamatea moons.

I have always been intrigued about the 'kai-ariki' modifier for today's moon. The literal translation 'chief eater' has been provided by some. Hina signals that the destructive element within all of us needs to be faced up to at this time. To my way of thinking this indicates a time to be aware that anger, aggression and violence can consume our own chiefly integrity.

Interestingly, puhi kai ariki is the name of a carved

figure, placed inside a ceremonial waka, at the base of the taurapa, the stern. In Tā Hekenukumai's waka *Hinemoana*, the puhi kai ariki is female. The manifestation of a female entity to guard the journey of the waka. A symbol representing the use of female essence as having dominion in the provision of safety.

One of the things I relish about our tūpuna, our ancestors, is their clarity in naming a day of the month to ensure we reflect on anger and danger. The words are such close relations in English too. Just look at the spelling. Danger is anger with a 'd'. The danger we pose to ourselves and others with our own destructive potential.

Looking deeply at the natural world, our old people could see the synergy between natural disasters and those qualities in each other. Our old people identified that this part of the month is one to be aware, and to be wary of destructive energies. The first of our Tamatea moons really hammers this home.

One such well-known event was the eruption of Tarawera in 1886. The famous Pink and White Terraces were gone for ever. The portentious vision of a ghost waka paddling across Lake Tarawera was reported by many observers, including visitors on board a tourist vessel on 31 May 1886, 11 days before the eruption of the mountain and the devastation that followed. That same day the water level of the lake rose, too. For the locals these were omens of disaster. They knew that this could mean Tama-o-hoi, an ancient being, imprisoned deep inside the mountain, was breaking free. On 10 June the sleeping volcano erupted. The flooding, earthquakes and ash destroyed whole villages. Many lost their lives. The violent eruption was seen by some as retribution for a transgression of the natural harmony.

Another example of the consequences of violence within the tikanga, the traditions of our old people, was for anyone who used violence or neglected to protect those within their system of safety. The expectations were high for anyone who was responsible for children and others under their protection. And if any were harmed, the repercussions were severe. The practice of muru, of taking compensation, was used to address these transgressions. Sometimes, this meant removal of all possessions, roles and status from those in charge.

Aroha Terry started a modern-day version of muru in the 1990s called marae justice.

Marae were used as the appropriate place for victims and alleged perpetrators and whānau to meet, and for them all to decide on the consequences as a collective. It was strangely controversial at the time, this return to the muru approach. But Aroha Terry was determined, and for many justice was delivered. Aroha's legacy lives on in restorative justice practices that continue to this day.

I will never forget travelling with Aroha in China in 1995 to the NGO* Conference on Women. It was a privilege to spend time with her and take care of her, as at times she was not well. We did have one hilarious encounter when she asked me to take her to the hospital.

The Chinese doctor did not beat around the bush. As soon as we sat down he said 'You are too fat.' And straight off the bat she replied with a raucous laugh, 'I know that, just give me some Chinese medicine to help me feel better.'

---

* Non-governmental Organisation

We talked a lot on that trip about how as women, Māori women, we hold on to our own special brand of anger, our hūngeingei, at the difficulties faced in seeking and achieving justice and protection for ourselves and our whānau. And that we sit in our anger, we fume, we brood, and that this contributes to our being unwell. Aroha has sadly passed away now, and I am mindful of being part of her legacy for honest and open ways towards healing these angry wounds. She encouraged me to seek stories to illuminate these initially unspeakable feelings as a way to help us all discover our own words.

Kurangaituku is one story that speaks to me of our female desires for control and possession. She was the famous birdlike female deity who lived in the ngahere, the forest of the Te Arawa rohe, in and around Rotorua. It is said that she took a young man called Hatupatu prisoner and kept him in her cave with her other treasures. I have wondered why she might have wanted to have him as her prisoner. Revenge? Seeing him as some sparkly treasure to hoard, to gloat about? As a delicious morsel of food? Maybe he was her natural prey?

Then he escaped. I wonder about the frenzy that must have overtaken her in trying to recapture him.

Tragically, she died in the process. And it must have been a grisly death, amid the hot mud and steam of Te Whakarewarewa. A potent story of female desire to possess and fury at that loss of possession, which didn't end well.

Riria, one of our female ancestors from Te Hiku o te Ika, the Far North, held onto her anger for many, many years. And she had good cause. She was left to drown when pregnant with twins by her then husband, when he decided he liked her sister better. She managed to swim to Matapia, an island named for a rock fissure that lets the light through, giving it the appearance of a 'shining face'. Hence mata, meaning face, and pia to shine. Riria raised her twin sons on the island. No doubt they grew up shaped by her rage and desire for revenge. When they were ready, they all returned to the mainland, where the twins killed their father and took over his mantle of authority as chiefs.

I think a lot about our stormy female traits on Tamatea kai-ariki. This is something our society finds particularly unpalatable. In my work as a court report writer I see this up close and personal. When I am exploring the forensic issues for our taitamāhine, our young women, that come into contact with the court, I see the cycles of pent-up female rage. Many of those involved bend over backwards to explain away and minimise this aggression. We don't want to see it. We don't like to call it for what it is. And the result is that our taitamāhine do not get the help they need.

Where does this aggression and destructive energy come from? It breaks my heart to say that most of these young women I have got to know through my work as a child and adolescent psychiatrist have developed their fearsome wrath because of being subjected to violence themselves. This has been taught. Our society is violent, especially towards women.

The young women I see in the courts are the tip of the iceberg. We have all been exposed to some sort of violence. Sadly, the easy access to porn for the young is adding a new dimension to distorted perceptions of what our rangatahi, our young people, regard as normal sexual behaviour. Mechanistic, often explicitly violent, this kind of sexual contact is now becoming the blueprint for rangatahi of all genders.

Hina invites us to dream uneasily today. We must

try to face our own anger, rage and desire to control and possess. These are less palatable aspects of all of our natures. And yes, te taiao, the natural world, can be brutal too. Our unacknowledged anger and frustration creates barriers for our journey through the rest of the month. It devours our integrity of purpose. Now is the time to take stock of our unpredictable natures. Own it. Talk about it, listen to the feedback of others. Expect and anticipate irritability or annoyance at the least.

Our wawata, our dream journey inward on Hina's Tamatea kai-ariki moon is remembering what makes us enraged and what we do with these feelings of hūngeingei. How do we hide them? Mask them, cover them over? How can we safely begin to defuse our own destructive energies? How might we reclaim our own puhi kai ariki, our female sentinel guardian, to lead our waka, our vessel safely through today's moon?

Tamatea wananga

Stand up to threat

Inā te mana o te tai ririki.

Such is the power of the neap tide.

We stand astride defiance and courage.

Our second Tamatea has many names.

Tamatea wananga is our name from home. Wananga is a word that denotes defiance and threat. Not wānanga, which is about deliberation, meeting and discussion. Such is the power of the tiny macron.

We are in a neap tide. He tai ririki, he tai ninihi, he tai kōwheuwheu, he tai moī. This is the first of two neap tides that occur each month, when Hina and Tamanuiterā are at right angles to each other. This sees Hinemoana, our ocean goddess, rising up and down, narrowing her gaze, not too far in, not too far out. She is focused.

Our wawata, our dreams, ruminate with her in this smaller area of the oscillating tide.

We wash back and forth with her, swaying with our mind's waves. Thinking and feeling, thinking and feeling. A turbulent energy emerges. We might feel under threat and this encourages defiance.

It is a day to scrutinise and reach a place where we can back ourselves. Stand our ground. Hina is here to help us deliberately, methodically smooth away any erroneous thoughts and feelings that form like the ridges on the beach, until what is left shines with smooth lucidity. Today is the day to be in this groove. This is how we respond to the wananga, the agitation of today.

It takes a lot of courage to withstand threat. I invite that courage into my dreams at Tamatea wananga. Brave dreams. Like Tamatea, we are now prepared for courage to emerge, especially when we feel threatened.

It is also a great day for netting kanae, mullet. A fish we love at home in the Far North. Reading the descriptions of our fishing prowess from earlier times is pretty awe-inspiring. The nets were often huge and were taken out by large groups. The first fish caught were always given back to Tangaroa, the ocean. Only as much as was needed was taken home. There was no waste.

There are practical applications for today. We are grinding out the necessary steps to catch enough to feed everyone. No matter if we have to repair the net, if we have to teach some of the younger ones how to hold and then set the net. No matter if, despite the appearance of settled waters, the under-currents are turbulent. We are feeling resourceful and connected to generations of our whānau, our family, who have done this back into the mists of time.

Our tūpuna, our ancestors, used the metaphor of netting fish a great deal. They emphasised the collective, the importance of working together. And I wonder about these kanae, mullet, delicious abundant nutritious sources of food for body and soul.

I see myself as one of our kanae, our mullet. In fact I have been called a 'kanae hama ki te rākau', 'a stunned mullet', by our beloved Waihoroi Shortland at my first Kura Reo in 2007. It is fair to say,

I couldn't understand much at all. And yet I have kept working to be caught in that te reo Māori net. Each time coming back a little less stunned.

This for me is at the heart of courage, that defiance under threat of this Tamatea moon. Dreaming our own determination into life, as manawa piharau, with the heart of a lamprey. A colloquialism referring to great stamina, just as the lamprey show in jumping up waterfalls to their spawning grounds.

How do we recognise our own audacity, our sheer dogged determination to confront peril, uncertainty and risk? For me, today is about not running away from who we are. Standing firm in what we believe in, that takes great stamina. Manawa piharau.

Do we even recognise ourselves when we stand brave and true in this era of social distancing, of social isolation? It feels brave to explore creative ways to build connection in these stricken times. Sometimes it feels easier to hide under the blankets and tell myself, it is not my problem to sort out.

But then the voices of my mother, Ina, and my grandmother, Annie, call to me. Soothing and strong. 'You are there representing us, and you are there for those who come after.' This is a time to withstand threat with our taonga tuku iho, our vast whakapapa resources.

Bring these forward to face off in this Tamatea wananga moon.

This first bulge of the persistent neap tide into Hina's dark side is really about guts, and guts are emotional. This puku of light. This Tamatea reminds us that what we care about, we protect. Pandemics, war and extreme weather emergencies strip away all the paraphernalia. We feel what matters. Let the determination of Hina's Tamatea wananga dream resonate within you today.

Tamatea ā-āio

Seek out tranquillity, rest and acceptance

Me he maonga āwhā.

Like the break in the storm.

Learning to say yes to rest.

Lying with my head on his chest, with my ear to my lover's heart, I rest.

It has been a long proverbial swim.

Today is a pause from the turbulence of processing anger, of fostering determination from generations gone by. And now, here I am, nuzzled within warm strong arms. Still learning to rest. Like my namesake, the original Hinemoa, it feels like I have swum a lake of living to find this love.

Tamatea ā-āio represents a time to seek out tranquillity, rest, acceptance. I find rest an emotional time. Letting go of the ‘doing’ and simply ‘being’ is something I admit I avoid, because it means complete surrender. Not something that comes naturally to me.

I imagine the original Hinemoa swimming across Lake Rotorua to her love, Tūtānekai.

A forbidden love. Unsanctioned by whānau and the mores of the day. She would have known the risks she was taking in going against the tide, against the wishes of those who had a plan for her, probably since before she was born. Swimming into the middle of the lake would have been a gruelling task by any assessment. Depite her being buoyed up by hue, by gourds, the journey from Ōwhata to the island of Mokoia is a long one in the dark of night. The currents and winds challenging her course. Challenging her resolve, her commitment.

I imagine her lit by Tamatea ā-āio. That is how Hina faces me tonight. Somehow her light reassuring and bringing our first Hinemoa safely to rest in my dreams.

The safety part is the critical bit of letting ourselves rest, isn’t it? I wonder about my own restlessness in attempts to find that peace. I am learning to accept this is really about my difficulty in feeling truly safe in relationships. It has been about a lack of trust. And trust has so many layers, don't you think? Once we have experienced betrayal, once we are forced to face lies and deceit, we bury that ability to surrender and truly rest so far down, deep in the lake. So we can't be hurt anymore.

My memory takes me back many years, to being with the tohunga, the healers at Waiōhau. Nestled in the lush valley of the Rangitāiki River, protected by the mighty Urewera.

Tūhoe country. Our group of Māori psychiatrists were there with Whaea Moe Milne and Phyllis Tangitu. These two extraordinary women were guiding us, these fledgling Māori psychiatrists. They took us around the community to listen to our own people, and to hear what was needed from us. It was on this hīkoi, this trip, that we were introduced to the healers.

I have never forgotten their kōrero. They told us that adjacent to their place of work, they created a small self-contained bedroom unit. And they always leave the door unlocked.

I asked them, why? With knowing looks, they explained, this is to ensure that weary travellers have a safe place to stop, accept and fulfil their need to rest. I cried at their generosity. I cried with recognition of my own weariness. My own need for rest.

This is the third of our Tamatea moons, the travellers' moons you might say, in homage to the great ones of old who carried that name. This is a time for hush and pause. The calm after the storm. Or as we say, 'me he maonga āwhā', literally like a fully cooked or ripe storm, the storm has come to its end. Accepting we must take an interlude at this time of the month. It might even be we need to have a nap. I know, I know. Naps are not a good idea to aid a good night's sleep overall. But maybe today is a monthly exception to that rule. We are all facing and absorbing so much stress and distress. We might find returning to the energy cycles of yesteryear a source of serenity, solace and repose in all the messy distractions of life.

How do we provide this for ourselves? By recognising today is our anchor point, our time out. The touch of a loved one's hand, a lingering eye contact, kissing an old family photo. This is how we leave the door open to our own place to lay our weary heads. Hina calls us to reach out for a safe resting place today.

Lying here, listening to the steady beat of my lover's heart lulls me into the pause I need.

Tamatea ā-āio. Saying yes to rest.

Tamatea whakapau

Review our assumptions

E kore e hohoro te opeope o te otaota.

The refuse will not be swept away so easily.

Our assumptions will not be so simply defeated.

It's Tamatea whakapau, and we are done.

We are completely used up. We found rest yesterday in Tamatea ā-āio. And from that resting place we can explore deeper layers fuelling our exhaustion. This is the ideal time to talk about this sapping of our energies. The destructive churning that may be invisible on the surface is the energy of today's moon. It is a time to be careful and draw close to those you trust. A time for reviewing those things that create turmoil for us.

Assumptions fit the turmoil bill for me.

Assumptions. They are exhausting and they frankly get in the way of living our best lives. They are the predictive texting of life.

We fall into the assumption trap. All the time. Assumptions are grumbling away just below the surface waiting for their chance. Thoughts like, 'I am not good enough, I'll never be good enough, I am a failure. I am a burden. Other people don't like me. Other people are laughing at me behind my back. I am a joke. I'll never have an orgasm.' I hear you say, 'Wait, what was that last one?' We will get to that.

I think of assumptions as half-baked beliefs. It's a belief where we missed some of the ingredients, we were in such a rush to get that assumption pie in the oven. And the rushing is a central point here. Why are we in such a rush to make our minds up about something?

I wonder whether, in the complexity of modern life, with the instant gratification demands we feel so acutely, we are unconsciously rushing to come to a resolution of the mind to cope with all that is going on in our lives. Maybe assumptions are the price we pay for all the things our minds are trying to manage. In evolutionary terms maybe our minds are still playing catch up.

So we create these shortcuts. We live through certain situations, we draw a kind of off-the-cuff conclusion, and then we apply what we have learnt to new situations as a bit of a time saver.
2 + 2 = 7, even when there is no evidence for this. And sometimes these assumptions lie dormant somewhere in the great filing systems of our minds, to be activated, often by some seemingly tangentially related situation. But because the whole thinking behind the assumption is a mess, we just keep tangling up those neural pathways. And so the assumptions are released. They come out into the open on the end of our tongues, in the way we look at and judge others and ourselves. They come out to sap the reality out of our decisions and to diminish us and our relationships. Who let those assumption dogs out? We did.

Let's take an inventory on Tamatea whakapau. A time to reflect on these negative thought patterns that weasel their way into our minds.

One biggie for me is that I did not want to be wrong about marriage. So after three marriages, my assumption was that I was a marriage failure. Not for want of trying, right?

I had some beliefs about marriage being forever, as many of us do. Despite lots of evidence all around us, and in our own lives, that this may not be the case. One of the reasons I stayed married so long is that I was determined to make it work, no matter what. This was on the basis that I was a failure at marriage. So, if I tried harder, for longer, things would be better. It was up to me. Exposing my underlying beliefs about it being my fault for not being good enough. These were my fears, based on experiences of feeling rejected in the past. That is how the assumptions played out in my head. So there I was, trying to be the best marriage partner. Marriage for me has been a place of facing many of my assumptions about myself. And at the kernel of that assumption, it is just so hard to admit when we are wrong.

What about some more intimate assumptions. A delicate area to explore. 'I am not going to have an orgasm. There will not be enough time. Never mind, my needs are not so important. If I ask for what I need I will be judged.' Our sexual health is such a critical part of who we are, and yet it is still shrouded in so many layers of assumption. Assumptions about gender and sexual orientation are slowly being unravelled and being brought out into the open, and yet there remains so much judgement, frank discrimination and persecution. Assumptions about sexual expression are deeply woven through our lives.

I have had only one partner in my life ask me, genuinely ask me, 'What do you need?' sexually. And, at the same time, they recognised it was hard for me to describe in the moment. I wonder if many people assume that their partners will ask and so don't realise that they can ask, too. This is a truly vital and liberating conversation. Even with gentle loving enquiry, this is an area that takes time to truly believe in and not hold fast to assumptions of judgement, or ridicule, or rejection. We may not find the words to explain what we need on the tip of our tongues. Finding those words and the courage to utter them takes time and patience. Jumping ahead and assuming everyone is expressing themselves fully might be less painful, less revealing in that moment. It might feel easier to just guess. And what is the result? Assumptions bumping up against assumptions. Is that really the intimacy we desire, we need, we want?

Facing those assumptions and their layers is painful, don't get me wrong. As I am writing this I am processing it again and it hurts. That is what the time of Tamatea whakapau is about for me. Recognising the power of the unpredictable. Oh, the irony. When you assume you have your assumptions sorted, think again. Ha, those assumptions can really morph themselves. I need to take stock every month. Our Hina moon provides a place for this.

A lunar reminder. Yes, Hina already has that in her diary.

Why do we do this to ourselves? On one level, we like to see patterns. Things that seem to fit together. And so our minds connect things that feel like a match with what we already believe. And then these thoughts, beliefs and assumptions become true for us.

They become part of us. Part of our identities and we cling to them for dear life.

Even though they were really only a match to other distorted thoughts.

Assumptions can function as a defence too. They protect us from the pain of an earlier experience. The assumption wall. The armour. We carry this protection forward. For me, creating that shield was done with the idea that having a partner was not for me. I projected my distrust, my skepticism as the deflector.

But my approach was flawed. Our assumptions might protect for a time, but they also hinder us from truly living. Truly feeling what is beyond the fears that drive the assumptions to keep those walls up. Those barriers that we create distance us from a deeper awareness, a deeper connection within ourselves and with others.

When we end up holding on tightly to these erroneous beliefs, this colours how we see the world. The colours begin to fade, they get pretty bland. We live in a strange, limited world of grey, making decisions based on fears.

How do we stop? How do we put the brakes on these assumptions and their ability to drain the colour out of life?

Today as our Hina rises in Tamatea whakapau,

remember to check your assumptions about yourself and others. This is the day we get to let our dreams free us from those ideas we held on to, without any proof they were real. Our wawata give us the freedom to practise letting go of all that exhausting erroneous mess. Done, we are finished with that. And, of course we get to review our progress, next time Hina brings Tamatea whakapau around. Because we know feeling fully free takes time.

3

Waiata ā-ringa

Toro mai tō ringa.

Reach out your hand.

Come closer.

Hina's next musical set, these next seven days, are our waiata ā-ringa, our action songs.

This is a week where we learn from the way we move and what our bodies do.

It is a time to experience our live-liness. Even when we are lying still we are in motion.

Our breath moves us and our heartbeats vibrate within us, our skin sweats and our eyes dilate.

'Toro mai tō ringa' is the opening line from a famous waiata ā-ringa from Te Hiku o te Ika, the Far North, my home. Written by an extraordinary man, Tā Kīngi Īhaka, it is one of our tribal anthems. It clearly identifies where we are from, and who we are. It speaks to the power of touch. The truth in friendship. The treasures of our ancestors. The pain of love for those who have passed on. Tā Kīngi was an extraordinary man, an orator, a man of the cloth, a broadcaster, a writer and composer, a Māori Language Commissioner. His legacy lives on in so many people and kaupapa, including this waiata ā-ringa.

One of the central messages of waiata ā-ringa is that our bodies have their own language, their own facts. They convey so much to us in the way they move.

Our bodies are constantly communicating. They are in the thick of their own narration, even with an almost imperceptible whisper. All the time. We are so alive with this dance, and the stories the dance steps tell. The undulations of our bodies match the swirling eddies of emotions and thoughts. Our feelings and physical movements so intimately interwoven. And our bodies' languages share a common vocabulary.

Writing each story on its own dedicated day and night has encouraged me to pay detailed attention to our bodies' movements and what they are trying to say.

Our vision, our breath, our hearts' beating. Our sexual energy, how our skin feels, our fertility and our laughter. Each with their own memoir. Some have dramas. Some have foibles to narrate. Some want to share their confessions.

Our bodies' stories can shed their own light on their relationship with our minds. Their side of the dynamic, their side of the story. How our physical forms reflect that flow of our wairua, that sacred energy that connects us to everything in the universe. That's their song.

This week is a time to feel the sinuous flow of our wawata, our dreams joining in as our bodies' musical autobiographies take centre stage.

Huna

Awareness of the breath

Me aro koe ki te hā o Hineahuone.

Pay heed to the dignity of women.

Learn from the breath.

It's a Huna moon tonight. Huna, concealed, hidden. These are the ways we think about the concept of Huna.

Huna is a time to be aware of our breath, and to grow that awareness. Finding ways to explore the extraordinary gift of breath, safe in this pearly light.

Here we are in our Huna cave, e hoa mā, my friends. The dark palm of night caressing Hina's glowing face. Held so gently, snug in this safe place to share some of her lessons.

Let's take the ancient advice, 'Kia noho puku i te rua

o Huna.' Let's remain in self-reflection in Huna's cave.

Our Huna moon always brings me back to the cycles of our breath. Not something we always pay much attention to.

Inhale, exhale. Expanding and contracting our chests with the flow of our Huna moon.

Our breathing creates movement, and the way we breathe gives us this vibrant energy.

The sway in our hips for today's waiata ā-ringa, for Huna's song.

I have been thinking about that tiny, almost imperceptible pause in our breath, the one where the breath is held at the top before its release. The breath is hidden there, waiting.

The lungs are filled with oxygen. That for me is a real Huna cave moment, the breath is held suspended, the exchange is happening hidden deep in our tiny alveoli.

That is the moment just before we expel carbon

dioxide, the waste products, the garbage.

Somehow our senses are heightened in that moment.

I want to pause in that state of suspended animation, that Huna moment, and talk about the cycles of who we are as women. Hineahuone was the first woman, the first human breath was hers. So when I focus on my breath in the Huna moon I always think about this genealogical line that connects me to Hineahuone and her breath. She was given that leadership role, without much choice. And aren't we all? We have got to know the landscape of leading as women, as mums, daughters, sisters, nieces, nannys, aunties, granddaughters over the years. Often our leading goes unrecognised. Our skills minimised.

I am remembering a time when a male colleague asked me whether I thought a female on our team was really ready for a new level of leadership, a promotion. I was incredulous to be honest. I told him what I thought he could see from her CV. What I thought he knew from the mass of evidence and recognition of her contributions, far and wide. She had been in leadership roles, whether she liked it or not, her whole adult life. I realised that he didn't see her. He didn't see value in all that she had contributed as a woman, beyond the peer-reviewed science journal articles, beyond the conference presentations. He couldn't recognise her community work, her support of whānau. That was invisible to him.

In that moment I noticed I was holding my breath. I was right up in Huna's cave. And it felt as though I was not in control of the quality of the air I was breathing. It was a not so subtle reminder that our proverbial oxygen can get shut off without any discussion or warning.

At any time. The air we breathe feels controlled by others sometimes.

These are the thoughts I hold in suspended animation today. To continue to digest them, to draw on the strength they give me to fight for clean emotional air. And for the freedom to fully expel the unhealthy, toxic waste of experiences, to move forward afresh.

To breathe that clean air again, to feel refuelled.

Hineahuone passes on her wawata, her dream for us in that Huna moment. Today we can connect with her first received breath and hold on. Hold on to our belief in knowing there is always a way for us to discover our own healing, on our terms. And to expel the detritus.

If only our thoughts and actions could always work as efficiently as our lungs in driving out what is not serving us, in providing that clarity of air in re-oxygenating our whole being.

Our Huna moon harks back to that first breath. 'Me aro koe ki te hā o Hineahuone', pay heed to the dignity of women. That first expansion of the lungs. Then the Huna moment, where the magic of life happened.

At Huna we can pay deliberate heed to those crucial milliseconds. That homage to the first woman. Feel that lilt of your chest and arms moving as you breathe, this is the music of our hā, our breath. Embrace this time of recognition of our female lineage, and gather together our thoughts in readiness for our next breath, and the next and the next.

Ariroa

The power of eye contact

He kaha kerekere tō te whatu.

The pupil of the eye has such intensity.

Look yourself in the eye.

Eye contact. Such a profound part of how we connect.

I remember the first time we made full sustained eye contact when we kissed. The clarity, the ariroa of that moment. Slow motion lightning striking. The magic of Hine Te Uira, the goddess of lightning, her light ran straight through me. Her sudden flash of white blinding my whole brain, rippling through my nerves, right down to my toes. Everything shining. It was like that moment when I am getting my eyes tested. When the imprint of the blood vessels in my retina stains my vision for seconds afterwards. This is a different kind of eye test.

Our pupils locking together like dials on a safe, opening our vaults.

That sudden jolt of awareness. In through dark tunnels. Undeniable clicking and fusing together.

I think about that moment. I return to the direct, clear way our eyes held each other, suspended in time. I felt you see into me. I felt your gaze touch me somehow. A different kind of touch. Your eyes touched me with their own invisible lips.

Now, wearing our masks, our eye contact is so much more pointed. I love to look at you. Our mouths, cheeks, chins, noses covered. Those distractions gone. Our eye contact so intense. The crinkling at the corners. I can tell, we are both grinning under our masks.

Your eye colour changes. Sometimes a shimmering pale bluey-green. The amber chocolate shades transformed. Candlelight from within seems to illuminate your irises. I imagine us as characters in my cartoon dream. Me, morphing into Hine Te Uira's arrow of lightning, shooting into your pupils' deep space portal. The vortex pulls me deeper, along the nerve trails that run from the back of your eyes, crossing over and weaving to the occipital lobe of your brain. Carrying Hine Te Uira's sheets of flashing light across the sky of your mind.

Delight fills me up. De-light. What a perfect word for this. Our eyes don't lie. I love the hīnātore, the phosphorescence. The spotlight suddenly opens that circle of light shimmering down onto the stage. Our truth exposed. The reveal of our eyes working their light magic together.

Sometimes I look at myself in the mirror. Really look into my own eyes and try to see what you see. It's never the same. I don't feel that shiver of lightning down my spine. But I do smile with the memory. I thank myself. Finally. I thank myself for being ready to be seen the way you see me. Surrendering to a new kind of ready transparency.

I notice how I don't actually look into my own eyes when I look in the mirror. I am looking at what I am doing, the hairbrush in my hair, the toothbrush on my teeth, or rubbing the moisturiser into my cheeks. So I have started a practice of deliberately looking myself in the eye. Trying to look inside. Checking in with myself.

In through my own pupils, traversing deep down into my own headspace. I think of these looks as lighting the way. Shedding light and clarity into my mind.

These are the seeds I plant today on Ariroa, this auspicious clear day. Planting connection seeds with my eyes. Why don't you give it a try?

Hotu

Exploring our hearts' desires

Whakatangata kia kaha.

Personify courage.

Follow your heart.

Hotu is a powerful kupu. A potent word. Embued with desire, longing, and even the chafing of resentment. Such is its rub.

It is a time to completely immerse ourselves in stories that remind us of our deepest desires. Those experiences that evoke strong feelings and remind us what we truly care about. The things that move us. This is the period of Hina's orbit for us to follow the urges of our yearning.

I think about all the movements of the heart itself. The heart muscle cells are unique in the way they connect, the way they grip each other. This gives them the ability to move in synchrony with the electric impulses that create our heartbeats. The squeezing of the upper and lower chambers. The filling and pumping. The valves and the turbulent rush of the freshly oxygenated blood flooding out around the body. All this happening without us thinking about it. And at the same time, something we are acutely aware of. Especially when we become aroused, activated, excited, when our heart speeds up. When our hearts miss a beat. Our hearts have their own musical reo, their own language.

The primal sense that shoots like an arrow, straight to my heart, is my sense of smell.

Certain fragrances, like my mother's perfume, take me back to chats in her bedroom when I was young. Cooking smells of hāngi remind me of some epic hāngi cooked at our local high school to celebrate Matariki, the Māori new year. The Hotu moon is the time of heart's desires and those potent scents draw me back to my inner courage. This is how Hotu encourages me today.

Hotu catapults my mind back to a Kura Reo, an intensive language school, at Te Aute College in southern Hawke's Bay in 2010. My heartbeat begins to quicken when I recall the glorious colourful paintings in the wharekai, the dining hall. The exquisitely adorned wharenui, the meeting house. I feel that warmth glowing deep in my heart. The warmth of our language learning. 'Tutungia te Hatete o te Reo', our anthem lilts back to me. Stoke the language fire. And all the pain and the longing that goes with igniting that path. The desire, our hearts aflame as we stumble along that rocky path, all gripped with the same affliction. That thirst to learn to speak with the tongues of our tūpuna, our ancestors. All of us consumed by a lust for our reo, our language, and all the complex emotions that come on that journey with us.

I treasure a photograph of Tā Tīmoti Kāretu and Te Wharehuia Milroy from that Kura Reo. Their close bond of brotherhood, so moving and inspiring. Their conspiratorial glances and smirks. Their keen watchful eyes aware of everything, every move we made, noting every inch we clawed forward on the reo path.

And at the heart of our stay is that magic whenua. The land we stood on. The land that held us in our reo slumber each night. Sending up its own heartbeat, up through the soles of our feet as we stood together and sang, that whenua-rhythm reminder to just put one reo foot in front of the other.

This whenua was gifted by Te Hāpuku and Ngāi Te Whatuiāpiti for a school to be set up at Pukehou in 1854. This is the land on which Te Aute College now sits. And as the school motto says, 'Whakatangata kia kaha', personify being strong. Stirring us on to be that strength of continuity from our forebears. Such a fitting gauntlet to be thrown down.

We felt that continuity of strength, that commitment to our reo in that place. The stories of that land seeped into us, helping us, literally grounding us.

I returned to Te Aute for an evening in the meeting house as part of the local book festival's events in 2021. A wall of emotion hit me as I reconnected to the stories of that place.

A coming home to the pangs at the heart of my reo journey. The delicious wafts of kai cooking in the kitchens. I felt my heartbeat synchronise with the beat of that land and all those who had stood there before me.

And there was another fragrance at play, touching my heart that night. Perhaps it was the Hotu moon, and the night air, and the whenua sending up clues from the ngahere, the forest, close by. My heart reached back to the love story of the exceptional young woman from that area, from that very whenua.

Māhinaarangi, smart, skilful and gorgeous. She was also known to be artful in waiata ā-ringa. Her love story is an epic tale. Māhinaarangi used the scent of raukawa leaves to signal her attraction to a young man named Tūrongo. She bravely passed close by him on several occasions so he got a good whiff of the raukawa perfume. But she remained elusive.

He couldn't see who she was. Intrigue was afoot.

'Early one evening, before the rising of the moon, she carefully sprayed raukawa perfume.' She spoke the words, 'Taku aroha e te tau; taku aroha!' 'My love, O beloved; my love', and ran off. Leaving him guessing, recognising his desire only by the fragrance of the raukawa. So says the retelling of the story in *Te Ao Hou*, in te reo Māori and English.*

---

* 'Mahinarangi and Turongo', *Te Ao Hou*, January 1953, p. 17.

Finally Māhinaarangi's identity was revealed. From there, it was all on. The lovers' ultimate union is celebrated and enshrined in the name of the mighty iwi, Ngāti Raukawa. Immortalising how the tribe got its name. The descendants of the extraordinary Māhinaarangi and Tūrongo. The tribal identity a poignant reminder of the power of scent in fuelling the heart's desire.

And because of this land and the gifts of this place of learning, my heart was able to read the passions and beauty of this story in our reo. The power of scent and the workings of the heart.

Our fragrant wawata, our dreams today propel such excitement of the heart. Our sense of smell transporting us to other times and places of love and desire. What aromas drive you wild, get your juices flowing, bring to life and personify that strength and courage? Today is a day to spice things up and utilise your olfactory prowess to enhance your heart's desires.

Māwharu

Female sexual energy

Wehe atu ki te rekareka.

An orgasmic high.

Find your cloud nine.

This is a moon of extraordinary energy. A powerful surging tide. We have been in a slow build-up. Laying the ground work. Finding precision. Suspended in that moment at the top of our breath. Nurturing our hearts' heat with sweet connection. Now we rocket upwards, unstoppable.

I love to watch how Hinemoana, the deity of the ocean, rises up alongside her mother Papatūānuku, Mother Earth. How high she rises during this tide. Pushing beyond the boundary of the beach up onto the grass. Higher and higher up into the valley of the bay where I live. Seeing our ocean stroking the contours of the land makes me wonder, how does it feel for our earth mother? Does she feel this as we do, like the sudden waves rushing up our legs at the beach? That massaging contact seems to signal how much the waves missed us.

Welcome to Māwharu.

Over the last three days, we have been preparing ourselves in anticipation of today's burst of energy. A spectacular time of the month when we can unleash our female sexual energy. Yes, that's where we need to go today. When I think of Māwharu I think of sexiness and great sex.

And don't we know how our female sexuality can be confronting not only to others, to other women, but to all genders, and ultimately to ourselves?

When I think of our tūpuna wāhine, our female ancestors who embody the mana, the respect and status of a beautiful sexual wahine, I think of Erenora Taratoa of Ngāti Raukawa. An appropriate reference, given the story of the origins of Ngāti Raukawa yesterday, in Hotu.

Erenora's lustre was such that it drew the envy and jealousy of other women. She was proverbially ripped to shreds for her potent sexual allure by her female peers. In response, Erenora composed an exquisite pātere, a vigorous rhythmic chant, where she unashamedly celebrated her sexual power.

Hers is a most extraordinary pātere, a musical retort: 'Poia atu taku poi' 'Swing far, my poi'. By way of the poi's elegant swinging action and rhythmic beating, this pātere tells the tales of Erenora's whakapapa, her tribal affiliations. And she talks candidly about travelling with her tara, her genitals, as her companion. She sings, 'māua ko taku tara', me and my vagina. 'Ka rawe rā māua ko taku tara ki te hāpai ewe ki ngā whenua'. See how my sex and I carry the afterbirth throughout the land. Erenora uses the pronoun 'māua', me and her, making her tara her sex, her guide, her chaperone, her bestie, on her travels.

I have read a few different translations of this waiata. Mostly they are a bit coy. You might say they are protecting our modesty. And that's all well and good. But, and I say this with care, doesn't that also continue to hide the great power of this woman's call to take pride in who we are, vaginas and all?

Does it strike you as hard to believe, even in this day

and age, that the idea of getting to know our own sexual organs is still seen as extreme, unnecessary or even perverted?

Many women don't even know that the place where urine exits the body is different from where menstrual blood and babies emerge (unless a Caesarean is needed). Many women have never looked at this part of their bodies. How do we balance respect for our bodies and our own self exploration? If we are not sure of our bodies' functions, how can we celebrate our intimate selves?

I wish I had known more about positive female sexual energy and these tūpuna role models, their waiata, these songs, when I was young. Their experiences, narratives, and celebration of our female forms would have imparted their strength for a better relationship with my body earlier in life.

I wove my sexual experiences into my partners' needs first and foremost, my needs reflecting theirs. What I have discovered in loving myself now and finding this connection with my own body is that I now have more to share with my partner. This is Erenora's gift.

Our next generations need to have safe experiences of their own sexual energy and power. And the freedom to express that.

Māwharu is that time to let our wawata, combined with those of our tūpuna wāhine, guide us. Their dreams coming alive in us. There is further we can go, we can feel more. There is more we need to feel.

Embrace Māwharu and her flood of energy. Time to be filled with pleasure. An orgasmic high. Wehe atu ki te rekareka!

Atua whakahaehae

Wounds of the past

Te kuku o te manawa.

The pincers of my heart.

I love you.

We expect this to be such a positive phrase. A moment of shared joy. The beginning of a new chapter.

But hearing those words can strike fear in the heart. Can't they?

We all live with a compilation, with a mix tape of 'I love you' songs that were not joyous at all. 'I love you' waiata that were loaded with lies. Hearing those words and knowing they were not true. Hearing ourselves uttering those words and knowing we were lying to ourselves, as well as to the one we were supposed to love.

He atua whakahaehae, a terrifying demon! What a strange and terrifying monster the words 'I love you' can be. Those words can really stab us in those vulnerable places where the pain is most excruciating. Cut us to the quick. Carving deep into old wounds.

The old 'I love you' torment. All those times we heard the words and they were really a cardboard cut-out of love. A pretence.

Hina has been building us up to this. Time to rip into the interwoven physical and emotional pain of past 'I love you's and learn from them. To my way of thinking, this is to prepare us for tomorrow's Ōturu, a time of great optimism. Another real high point of emotional energy in our month.

But how to navigate this multi-layered pain, how to gather insights from under our atua whakahaehae? First we must examine our deepest love injuries.

We have been taught to seek love, we are nurtured with that quest in mind, and we come to believe that we are incomplete without it. Sometimes the words spill out. Sometimes we can feel pressured to say the L word.

We can tell someone we love them, but there is no guarantee we actually know what we mean by this. Let alone if the other person really understands what we mean. Do we know how to love and be loved? Are we ready for the challenge of love?

We love the idea of love. Maybe we feel we need to be 'in love'. We crave that idealised connection with another. We want to be wanted, to be needed. We want that elusive, and exclusive feeling of something rare. And yet saying those words is something we learn to be extremely careful about. There are a few songs written on the topic. I bet you have your favourites.

There are many waiata aroha, love songs. Many by female composers about love lost, about being rejected for another. Our moon is often a companion in the waiata.

'Tērā te marama ka roko-mahuta ake i te pae

Ē, rā runga ana mai o te rae ki Kohi ē

He ripa tauārai ki te tau rā nā te ngākau ē.'

Behold the moon rising over the ranges.

Climbing upwards from beyond the brow of Kohi

The barrier to the loved one I long for.*

Atua whakahaehae comes after the massive build-up to Māwharu, the explosive rush of sex drive, followed by the possibility of fertilisation on Ōhua. Atua whakahaehae, right in between, is the day for really putting our hot messes under the microscope and not holding back. An emotional blood-letting.

I imagine our old people who practised whakahaehae, the slashing of their chests when in deep emotional pain at the death of a loved one. Scratching deep into the skin until the blood ran free.

What does it mean for you to say, 'I love you'? How does your skin respond? What does it mean when you hear those words? Do the words instil a sense of being loved, in the way you need that love? Or do you immediately doubt and feel unworthy of love?

This is the day and night for those brutally honest wawata, those dreams to roam free.

---

* *Ngā Mōteatea* pp. 194, 195.

To question our own personal back stories to these words and the monster they can create for us. To ask ourselves, what do we want the experience of loving connection to feel like from now on? What are the right words, and how to say them? Let's massage these new words into our skins.

Ōhua

Fertility

Ko wai ka kite i te hua o te kuaka?

Who has ever held a kuaka's egg?

Trust the process.

Ōhua, a day about the fruits of our labours.

Hua is our word for fruit. So today is about wawata that help us discover ways we trust in that fruition. The products and progeny, the abundance. Particularly in our body's subtle movements today.

Hina's Ōhua face looks a bit like an egg. Her presence today vibrates with fertility. Bulging, fecund, rich with that air of results. Close to full exposure, light so bright.

But not quite fully revealed. We must wait here before rushing on to Ōturu and Rākaunui.

It seems only right that two days after an orgasmic high and contemplating our own personal love monsters, we contemplate the consequences; we are glowing, radiating with the flush of abundance.

'He rā tino pai mō te hakatō nei', it says in our Te Aupōuri Okoro, our local moon chart.

A good day for planting. Yes indeed. Seeds may well have been planted and now results begin to develop. Often invisible at first.

Ko wai ka kite i te hua o te kuaka? Who has ever seen a kuaka's egg, a godwit's egg?

A famous whakataukī, a proverb from home. Our kuaka, our godwits held such fascination for our old people. A lesson about trust is presented.

Kuaka eggs are not something we see in Aotearoa, because the kuaka breeds elsewhere. We do not need to see these eggs or hold them in our hands to know what is inside, or that they exist. The eggs will grow and will hatch as they are designed to do.

There is a trusting energy when we think about the invitation to just let that growth, let that expansion of who we are becoming do its thing. Unseen, just like the movement of the growing bird inside the mysterious egg, also obscured from view.

How can we find a way to trust that the results of that growth can be seen and felt later, at the right time?

Like the kuaka, our human eggs are hidden too.

We do have hints that our human eggs are being released from our ovaries. There is the pain of 'mittelschmerz' — a German word used to describe the mid-cycle pain associated with ovulation. There are tangible changes in the viscosity of our fluids, the body's temperature increases, our breasts may be a little tender. And some people feel more sexy at this time.

And yet our human eggs stay hidden, moving towards our whare tangata, our womb, and the moment of fertilisation is most often a mystery that we are not aware of.

Today is about those imperceptible movements within us, movements of eggs inside ovaries, migrating along their preordained pathway, through the fallopian tubes perhaps, or nestling into the womb.

It is a time to contemplate that secret steady flow of blood. The transmission of signals between nerve cells. The quiet flushing of lymph. Finger-like waves, like anemones in the gut.

These hidden waiata ā-ringa, these action songs, bear their own fruit. We must be patient and wait today.

Observe what is happening with these delicate and yet significant stirrings. The wiriwiri within us. The wiriwiri, a trembling motion of the hands seen in our performances of traditional dance forms.

We are preparing for a new energy. Adapting in readiness for a new level of Hina's brightness and scrutiny.

Our wawata, our dreams, are about what we foresee and the power we experience in biding our time. Waiting patiently for the fruits of our labours to become visible.

Let these fluttering wawata from our bodies' gentle

hidden movements open us to trust this dance.

Trust that the fruits of our endeavours are not always so clear, at least at first.

There remains some shadow on Hina's face. Wait, all will be revealed.

Ōturu

Female humour

Me he Ōturu ngā karu.

Beautiful eyes, like the radiant Ōturu moon.

Embrace all of your beauty.

Ōturu is a moon of optimism and planning. So much light, we are almost there, almost at Rākaunui, our full moon.

We see Hina's face from afternoon until before dawn. She is in a whimsical mood, keeping a little bit of her face back, cheekily hiding that last fraction of herself for one more day.

Our Ōturu moon is a time for the use of humour. Now is a time for teasing, giggles and full-bellied laughs. That tickling youthful glee bubbling up, carrying us on the crest of that wave, to the big reveal, the full force of Rākaunui. Ōturu is a time for the witty repartee of our tūpuna, our old people, especially of our wāhine, our women.

There is a particular kōrero, back and forth banter between two esteemed Māori women, that I love to mull over today. They are the revered Hinepuariari and Rongomaiwahine. High-born mana wāhine. Strong, feisty, sassy as they come. Unafraid to tell it like they see it. Literally. Their commentary centred on the genitals of a well-known tāne. The man in question was Kahungunu. He is the famous eponymous ancestor of Ngāti Kahungunu, the tribal group bearing his name, and one of our Māori world's most illustrious lovers. And according to these women in his life, he was rather well-hung.

It is reported that his wife at the time, Hinepuariari made the comment, 'Kāore hoki tērā te hanga o taku tāne, kāore e rūpeke mai ana, takoto noa mai te nuinga i waho.' You could say, 'My husband is so well endowed, most of him remains outside of my vagina when we make love.' She leaves little to the imagination.

This statement was then reported to Rongomai-wahine, a woman who would also become Kahungunu's wife down the track. Like a comment on social media, Rongomaiwahine let it be known, 'Nā te mea anō rā he kōpua pāpaku, mehemea e taka mai ana ki te kōpua hōhonu a Rapa e tūwhera atu nei, pokopoko ana ia ki roto.' In English, this can translate as, 'That is because it is a shallow vessel; if however, he were to fall into the deep pool of Rapa, which is wide open to him, he will indeed drown.' Drown with pleasure, I suspect she means.

What I love about the exchange between these wāhine is the unflinching strength and confidence about their sex. The size of their vaginas in relation to the size of a man's penis a subject they felt at ease to discuss with more than a little witty repartee. Our ancestors were not prudes. Their relationships with their bodies and the bodies of others were steeped in a completely different world view of sacred respect.

He tapu te tinana. The body is sacred. These wāhine were able to make these rather teasing, jocular remarks about the intimate fit of their bodies. I am struck by the contrast with our contemporary female convos. I have not witnessed us, so-called 'modern' women, trading comments about our vagina size, have you? The idea of a vagina being a such a huge space that a man's penis could drown there, and enjoy it, might not resonate as a positive thing with some contemporary women.

Confidence about our bodies and our vaginas being such a fundamental part of who we are, is something that, in our experience, modern society is actively attempting to strip away from us. Keeping women in a place of such emotional vulnerability and fear is an essential part of social control. Misogyny is alive and well. Fostering worry about the functioning, the smell, the moistness, the taste, the size and shape, the surrounding hair, of our vagina means we are exposed to a rejection of our most intimate selves by society. The proposed solution is commercial. Buy products and services to adjust, to literally block up or mask the flow of being female. We are taught that we are not clean.

The whakataukī or proverb says, 'Me he Ōturu ngā karu,' like our Ōturu moon, true beauty can be seen in the eyes. Ōturu is a time for those laughing eyes, open wide, joyful, unafraid to simply be. Whatever the characteristics of our vaginas.

I find myself chuckling with the cheeky glow of Ōturu in my wawata dreaming today. I feel that vagina-deep hilarity and I laugh in the face of every put-down of my body. I relish the openness of our tūpuna wāhine. Ōturu is the time to let that laughter bubble up from deep inside, and I can almost hear Rongomaiwahine and Hinepuariari laughing with me. Care to join us?

4
Poi

Rākaunui and Rākaumatohi

'Poi e, whakatata mai.'

'Oh my feelings, come closer.'

This is the opening line from the chorus of one of the most famous songs about and for poi. Written by the inimitable duo of Dalvanius Prime and Ngoi Pēwhairangi and famously perfomed by the Pātea Māori Club*. This song and its use of poi had the specific goal of promoting our language, our modes of expression, our way of thinking and feeling, our Māori identity. Their wawata, their dreams for our rangatahi to discover purpose and joy in being Māori through poi, came to life.

These two nights, when Hina is full, look just like our beloved poi. These almost identical twin spheres resemble huge celestial poi themselves, held in the hands of a massive, heavenly performer over two days and nights.

Poi have their own whakapapa. Their own origin stories. Tānemahuta, the deity of great forests, is

* Patea Māori Club, 'Poi E', Maui Records and Jayrem Records, 2000.

the ancestor of both Raupō and Harakeke, reeds and flax, which together form the original materials used to make poi.

Our two full Hina nights, both named Rākau, a word for tree, also signal whakapapa links, lineage from Tānemahuta.

Poi. Our word for this unique art using the simplicity of round balls suspended on a cord. Watching them pirouette in expert hands is jaw-dropping. And from afar, to watch the dizzying dexterity with which exponents can make those white dots swirl in concert is a magnificent sight.

The word poi indicates the objects themselves and the act of using them, too. They accentuate and embellish the body's movements. Poi are used by all genders. One can be held in either hand. A few extraordinary experts can hold two or three together all at once. They can have short or long cord lengths and can be double, triple or quadruple stringed.

Poi have been used since time immemorial by our people to enhance flexibility and strength in the hands, wrists and arms. The poi dance movements illustrate the artistry of both beauty and flirtatious seduction, as well as a means of training for the precision and durability required for combat. Often poi were used to express the circuitous pathways of affections described in the words of a song.

My Aunty Rata was known to be pretty hot stuff with the poi. She is mentioned on the sleeve of the long-playing record I have from her days with my Uncle Rex in the NZ Army 'haka party' group. Poi bring back sweet memories of my darling Aunty.

These two nights are a special time to bathe in these poi headlights on full beam. Birth stories and tales of renewal come to the fore. Enjoy the excited rhythms and energies of our next two nights, come and dance with Hina's poi.

Rākaunui

Light reveals all

Āhuatia koia te marama.

The moon is exactly full.

Bathe in the light of Rākaunui.

Rākaunui, huge glowing light sabre that you are,
I feel your intense strobes of light on my face.

Your searchlight follows as I leave the inky velvet contrast of the dense bush around home, heading for the ocean. I want to see you shine your aroha, your love, on Hinemoana tonight. I let my eyes softly close and feel you through the skin of my eyelids. Rākaunui has such a piercing gaze, pushing the rest of the sky deeper into its own obscurity.

Rākaunui the fullest moon, the greatest light. How you got your name is something I dream about. Maybe it is because your light spreads as if from the trunk of a great tree with a far-reaching light-canopy of branches and leaves. You illuminate every tiny frond, like fairy lights dancing at a party. So then, this is an ideal night for a get together. I imagine our old people making sure to plan their celebrations around this night and her twin Rākaumatohi, tomorrow. What better time than this for those ceremonies of the sacred union between two people? A special time for pākūhā, wedding feasts. Pākūhā resonates as a word for darling, with some racy overtones too, the kūhā being the thighs. A word that speaks to thighs touching thighs. That's what we expect on a wedding night after all, right? Rākaunui is our celestial celebrant. He tai a Kupe, this is the time of our spring tide. Celestial forces are aligned. We feel the universe unite us tonight.

Rākaunui, you compel us to make oaths that speak to our inner truth. Our own nuptial vows, oaths that connect us. You make things so clear. Nothing can hide from your all-seeing eye. You remind us to face our bonds with the natural world and to see our place in it, no excuses. The extremes of light and dark, a marriage of equals tonight. And the power of the spring tide provides those messages as the dawn edges into the sky. Touched by this spotlight as I stand there on the beach of my dreams. My heightened sense of simply being. Standing sentinel. We stand with our own histories and foibles, all under the pointed gaze of Rākaunui. Somehow being in this light makes me feel a lightness, a kind of floating sensation. Being a tiny part of this great flood of radiance. Sensing the apex of the magnetism between Hinemoana and the light above us. Being in that force field.

I travel back in time to the birth of my daughter. As soon as she was born, we lifted her onto my chest. She first opened her right eye. The piercing gaze of her eye into mine is something tattooed in my memory. My own Rākaunui high-beam moment.

Rākaunui is the time to focus on our absolutes. Our legacies, what do we leave behind with our children and their children? This is the reckoning. They are who we answer to, our future deal breakers. This is the one day a month to take time to soak in the Rākaunui aroha. The potent, fierce drive to connect and commit to loving ourselves, others, our planet, all at the same time. It is time to peel away all the fluff, the packaging that we have created in our lives to cope, in order to soften the cruelties of our world. How did we collect so much detritus? All of our distractions and avoidance. Our scarcity mindset, we come from the belief there will never be enough, that *we* will never be enough. Tonight is the night to look long and hard into ourselves in the full beam of Rākaunui. And to make the call, to draw that line in the sand.

Sand.

Desert sands on Rākaunui, forever forged in my mind. Rākaunui takes me back to the desert sands of Dubai. I was finishing this book while I was part of a rōpū contributing to Te Aratini, the first indigenous festival of ideas at a World Expo. Te pito o te Ao, at the centre of the world, hosted by Sheikh Omar and his family in the desert near Al Labsah. Out of those terracotta sands rose our incandescent Rākaunui. Majestic and all seeing. Hina's myriad Rākaunui branches of light, her own aratini, lift me up and take me back across the world every month. Renewing my vows to that place and to those people. And to our caravan of global Māori, revisiting the ancient pathways of Māui.

Rākaunui's luminosity is a feast. The bounty of these nourishing connections is our kai, our food. There is more than enough. It is a time to be outside in the elements, to force ourselves to be in nature. On the waves of ocean or desert. Riding the undulations of earth. Time to put ourselves under Rākaunui's scrutiny. We cannot hide tonight. Surrender to the intensity of Rākaunui. Let that piercing light dive right into you, feel that direct unflinching gaze. Let that light reveal all of you. See and be seen, inside and out.

Rākaumatohi

Vibrant preparation

Moea tō poi, moea tō taiaha.

Sleep with your poi, sleep with your taiaha.

Be prepared.

Rākaumatohi. The twin. The second poi.

My wawata, my dream, takes me back to the time of another tohi.

A tohi is a ceremony conducted to establish and restore harmony and to convey success in life's endeavours. To prepare us for a new chapter in life. I see our group gathering at the water's edge. Naturally drawing closer to each other. Our feet sharing the water, icy fresh from the hīrere, the waterfall. The droplets flying up in sprays, like wild tears. Propelled into the air by the rhythmic movements of our kaiako, our teacher. He wields the sapling branches like wings. Dipping them first into the pool and then flicking the water overhead to purify us. Moths flutter in and out. A symbol of our musical goddess, Hineraukatauri, here with us to celebrate our new beginnings.

And with this Rākaumatohi ceremony we unleash a torrent of energy. Hina's night waterfall. That crashing wall of watery light.

Our tohunga, our esteemed expert, recites the ancient incantations. He calls down into the depths of our genealogy, bringing our ancestors' voices upwards, breaking the surface of the pool. Their words, their poetic rhythms, recounting the layers of our collective bonds. Guidance that glides so easily towards us with the cascading waters. These ancient relationships and their reciprocities are reawakened.

And it is loud. The water gushing inexorably down. The thundering weight roars in our ears. The vibration of that water resonating with this total cleansing and renewal. It is not gentle. It is a pummelling. And it does not stop. Deep within, I hear the matohi, a special haka performed only by men. I feel their passion and hear it echoing inside the water.

The fearsome prowess of our men. Strong, united, vibrant and joyful. Our generations of men, our sons, proclaiming the need for healing. Our men feeling that water releasing their burdens.

How to harness this Rākaumatohi energy today to set us up for the second half of the month? The restorative rebuilding, reviving and reconciliation of past roles, beliefs and behaviours. How can we bring all that to our mind's waterfall to be washed away? To find the vigour, the vitality, to haka those expressions of healthy male energy?

Our spirits rise with our renewed responsibilities to be who our ancestors dreamed of. To be their representatives alive right now. We are forever part of this sacred ritual, from here on in. We are marked with it. It has seeped in through the skin, through the shared moonlit breath. It vibrates in the pounding of our hearts.

Hineraukatauri, our goddess of music and of traditional instruments, holds the baton. She is conducting the music of the waterfall, the emerging haka. Hineraukatauri is music's queen in our natural world. And my thoughts naturally turn to our own, Dame Hinewehi Mohi and her daughter

Hineraukatauri, and the music therapy centre that bears her name.

A place where people of all ages immerse themselves in the healing that is inherent within music. Music washes over us, with the power of the waterfall, and its own commanding haka. We feel the collective vibration with our cells. Our blood rushing to tune in.

This drumming water and haka at Rākaumatohi, this is our music today.

Let your dreaming tune in to this frequency of energy. A new way to wake ourselves up. Be sure to get into the water. In your shower or into a river, the ocean or, if you are lucky, a waterfall. Plan something that really excites you today, live a little, let your hair down. Our second poi night begins our transition into haka. An omen of our next bracket of haka moons. Feel that waterfall roar within you in the brilliant light of Rākaumatohi.

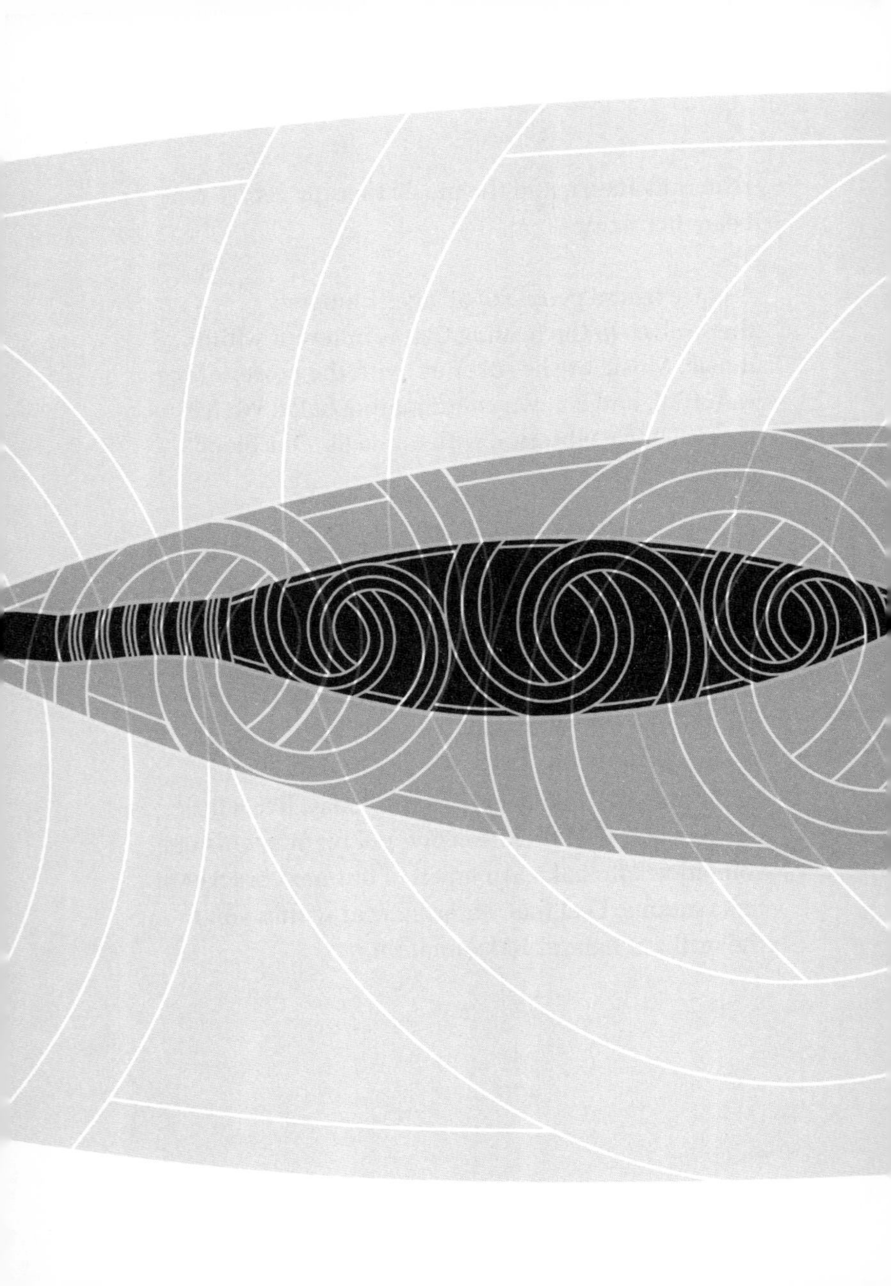

5
Haka

E ako au ki te haka
E ako au ki te ringaringa
E ako au ki te whewhera
E! Kāore te whewhera
E ako au ki te kōwhiti
E! Kāore te kōwhiti
E kōwhiti nuku, e kōwhiti rangi
E kōwhiti puapua, e kōwhiti werewere
E hana a tinaku . . . e!

I learn to haka
I learn to explore with my hands
I learn to open wide
Not to open wide
I learn to twitch
Not to twitch
Pulsating upwards, pulsating downwards
My vagina throbs, my vagina fibrillates
A haven of lingering warmth[*]

These are said to be the words of the very first haka. The inaugural 'we mean business' performance of challenge.

---

* T. Kāretu, *Haka: Te tohu o te whenua rangatira / The dance of a noble people*, Reed, Auckland, 1993, pp 15, 16.

It was performed by women, sent on an extraordinary mission. A cunning plan to identify the man who murdered and then ate a pet whale. His identity would be revealed using the power of their haka. If you want to get a deceitful killer to smile, this was the way to do it.

These women were sent by Tinirau to find Kae, a man Tinirau believed had eaten Tutunui, his pet whale. The women's performance needed to make Kae smile, revealing the well-known gaps in his teeth. It is said their haka was such effective entertainment that Kae's smirk did indeed betray him, revealing the telltale gap-toothed grin, perhaps some residual evidence of his whale meal stuck in between them. Needless to say, things didn't end well for Kae.

We now are entering what is, for me, Hina's time of haka.

Tānerore, deity of the haka, has so much to share with us over the next five days and nights. There is a concentration of energy in the air. The shimmering heat that emanates from the road. The hot mirage of haze is our new set point after the steely gaze of the Rākau twins, in our journey with Hina.

Tānerore's haka serve so many different functions. If you have ever been lucky enough to attend Te Matatini, the national competiton of Māori performing arts, you know what I mean. These performers are at the top of their game. Their haka send shivers down your spine. For performers of all genders, haka is perhaps some of the most electrifying and awe-inspiring of all of our performance art forms. And yet haka is so much more than performance. It is a central aspect of our Māori identity. The haka can provoke, it can express a clear challenge. It can be the ultimate welcome. Haka celebrates and marks special occasions. Haka conveys our stories of loss, anguish and death. Haka has its own unique language. Haka forces us to stand our ground. Haka is a site of resistance and resilience. Haka is a way of life.

So let's feel the shift down in the diaphragm, yes, time for some belly breathing. Strengthening our resolve to grapple with some of the big questions. Our losses and grief. Our female roles and responsibilities. Our aging. There is a deepening throb in this pulsing haka rhythm. Coming right up out of the whenua. I feel our narrowing of focus on Papatūānuku, Mother Earth.

Hina's next five days and nights invite haka into our wawata, our dreams. Themes are repeated. Drilled into us. It is a time to welcome powerful creative solutions.

Just like the ingenious haka strategy that revealed the truth about who ate the whale.

Let our haka bracket expose just what we need in Hina's light over the next five days.

Takirau

Energy shifts

Kia taiheke a Pātūpoho.

Let the diaphragm descend.

Feel the intensity of the emotional shifts.

Taki is a fascinating and multi-layered first part of Takirau, Hina's name today.

'Taki' often indicates 'many' at the beginning of words. Perhaps giving us shades of the many leaves and many layers, the many rau. The word taki is also used to describe things coming into view, including the rising of stars in the sky, such as Te Taki-o-Autahi, also known as the Southern Cross.

I love discovering these nuances of our language, the ways words touch each other's stories. I think a lot about how words relate to each other. They have their own whānau, their own close and distant relations, their own whakapapa or lines of descent. The secret life of our words. Today is a time to savour the meaning of these words. And to discover the way they challenge us to look deeper, down into their many layers of meanings, and how these meanings make us feel.

Now, we shift to a phase where energies are percolating. The many aspects of Takirau collecting into one. Drawn powerfully together. Even this small change is noticeable. Immediately after the pair of unforgettable poi nights, we feel the myriad ripple effects as we change gears. A distillation is occurring. Maybe this explains the name Takirau, as the dimmer switch on Hina's Rākau nights gradually winds the light down. Ever so slowly.

I have noticed I can often feel a bit 'kōhangaweka', as they say, at Takirau. A bit all over the place. This is such a great term, which comes from the untidy nature of the nest of the weka, one of our native birds. I wonder if it has to do with processing the aftermath of so much energy, inspiration and ideas that flow from our Rākau nights. Working out how to prioritise where and how the ideas and inspiration connect. What to embark on first.

My tendency is to get a bit overwhelmed and then rush to shut this process down, rather than sit with the turbulence as things subside slowly within me. I feel the need to control, perhaps because the shift can feel a bit full on. I know for me this drive to package up and to organise is premature. In fact, I miss out by not learning to sit with the gradual concentration of all the convoluted, jumbled-up feelings and see what emerges naturally. The way the energies become unified, and level out, has its own natural pathway. More free-flowing and revealing.

Today feels to me like the tiny rivulets of coffee as you push the plunger down, escaping from the perforations on the filter. A coffee-plunger haka if you will. These tiny, potent streams of energy are necessary for creating the perfect concentration of the finished coffee. And as the plunger drops down it creates this perfect confluence of waves necessary to make the coffee. If you push too fast, coffee spills out of the top and makes a mess. Imagine someone trying to hold the plunger in place, halfway down, to prevent it fully going to the bottom. That gives you a picture of what I try to do emotionally. With the plunger halted, the coffee doesn't have a chance to fully merge with the water to create the fullest of flavours. I miss out on the full effect of the change in energies, the more I try to resist. What I have learned is to let these Takirau dreams remind me to accept and let go of the drive to control the process.

It is the beginning of a period of the month to be aware of how we react when energy is compressing, fusing, becoming full-bodied. And then to learn from these responses.

Maybe you can relate to what I tend to do, trying to hold the energy in place, rather than surrendering, knowing this is part of Hina's natural waning process.

I have learned to let the music help me with this shift in energy. As the lights start to become slightly muted it is only natural that Hina's music shifts, too, maybe a bit of a minor key change? Hineraukatauri was with us yesterday. And today the woman I hold in my dream, my wawata, is Hinewirangi Kohu-Morgan. We first met in 2007 in the Atawhaingia Te Pā Harakeke programme. She has taught me so much over the years. One thing that resonates with me in Takirau is her love of our traditional Māori musical instruments. Hinewirangi makes these instruments by hand, and she plays them. She passes on her extraordinary mātauranga, her wisdom. She once taught us to make some from clay. I still have these treasures at home. Thinking about Hinewirangi reminds me to be in my body and especially to be aware of my diaphragm. To feel that internal muscular power. That is where I feel the breath-plunger sinking right down to. That is where the gravity of breath seeks its source.

I hold my hand to my diaphragm and breathe into that deep part of my body, feeling all those branching lung spaces filling right down to their depths. All that oxygen powering its own haka, my own dance of challenge. This is my practice at Takirau. Try this for yourself as we move with that steady reliable cadence of this part of Hina's journey.

Let your diaphragm do the work as you learn to wait for your emotional plunger to sink right down to where it needs to go this month. Put on some music today as you feel that turbulence. Watch a stirring haka, feel the pressure of those rhythms intensify in your body. Let go of worries about being in tune, sing along to songs in the car, in the shower, with the whānau. What music can you make to accompany Hina's shift in energy today?

Oike

Caring for Papatūānuku, our Mother Earth

Ūkaipō.

Our mother's milk, our land, our mother earth.

Come home to who you really are.

Oike is the time for wānanga, for gatherings where we exchange and learn, and for looking after Papatūānuku, our earth mother. Our Takirau plunger has brought us down to earth. Now it is time to explore our relationship with the very soil we stand on.

A thirst for knowledge is an important driver on this Oike moon.

Oike is the calling of our ūkaipō every month. A call to renew our vows to our earth mother and all her creatures. Our litmus test for reclaiming our kaitiakitanga, our guardianship role. It is the kaitiaki identity that calls to us from our ancestral lines. This is the genealogical technology to map our way back home.

Ūkaipō. What a word. And it means many things. A source of sustenance, mother, true home, origin.

Ki te taha o tōku ūkaipō ko Te Aupōuri tōku iwi.

I descend from Te Aupōuri on my mother's side.

This concept of ūkaipō, so much synthesised within one word. 'Ū' being breast, 'kaipō' meaning to feed in the night. The mother's milk that feeds us and gives us comfort, especially poignant at night.

The beauty of our language paints such a vivid picture, and brings to life the feelings of home, the warmth and comfort. That breast-fed closeness that some of us were lucky enough to experience. Skin to skin, cheek to our mother's breast. Hearing our breaths synchronise with her heartbeat.

This is the thinking and wisdom passed down by our tūpuna, our ancestors, who knew the critical importance of living in harmony with Papatūānuku. The intimacy and necessity of our own mother's nourishment is mirrored in our relationship with our earth mother. Without that relationship, we cannot survive. Ūkaipō.

And yet the paradigm we live in, the one that still controls and determines our relationship with Papatūānuku, is so very different. We have become part of a strange and destructive self-serving world view. In the process we have lost our ūkaipō.

Reclaiming this essential part of ourselves means first facing the very real pain we have caused ourselves in the process. This is pain that stems from our disconnection from our earth mother and from the part we continue to play in her destruction. Our wellbeing and the wellbeing of our taiao, our natural world, are one and the same. When we hurt our mother earth we hurt ourselves.

Our identity has become dependent on dominating our planet. We derive our value from our ability to take from her whatever and whenever we want, however we choose, with no mind to the consequences. Economic unit identity rules. The greater the profit the better. All part of the illusion of our planet's infinite resource and ability to rejuvenate.

How have we coped with this strange alien identity? As Papatūānuku's descendants, as part of the natural world, as living beings who are intrinsically connected, we needed to find ways to numb the shared pain of the atrocities, the mutilation. We had to wall off our connections to Papatūānuku. We had to maintain a certain magical thinking that we could sever those ties and survive. Our whakapapa, our genealogical links to our whenua, our land, had to be masked and hidden. For us to maintain this way of being, a painful price must be paid. We created a myth of our own separation, our otherness, our superiority. We justified our arrogance. This is at the core of how we were able to decimate her, poison her with chemicals and override her harmonious systems.

This estrangement is at the heart of our mental and spiritual agony, our profound grief.

Which is now inescapable. We can't hide what we have done and who we have become any more.

Oike, the name of today's moon in our Māori lunar calendar, is a time to focus our curiosity and self-awareness on our false and ultimately self-harming identity. Yes, it hurts and it is exhausting. And yet here is a day of the month that provides a fitting energy for these reflections, and for a shifting back to our healthy identity. A return home to our true selves.

And we need to anticipate denial, justification, minimisation, intellectualisation.

Our defences grow back like weeds, like mental mothplant. Let's see those mental invaders for what they are. Let's hold on to the energy of Oike as we work to discover the responsibility kaitiakitanga entails. We need this regular monthly kaitiaki review of where we are up to.

I look to follow the red aerial roots of the pōhutukawa. They know to grow down to the earth. Back to the earth memory, back to their bones. Those tiny knowing filaments, persisting despite the winds blowing them from side to side. They trust in that gravitational pull.

They are ready to curl up in Papatūānuku's sustenance and strength. I look to those air roots for inspiration at Oike. My curiosity to know more about my true self has sometimes felt like I was blowing around in the wind. Drifting, as these tiny delicate strands seem to. Watching those sacred threads reminds me to trust the pull of that ancestral gravity, drawing me back home to my ūkaipō. The shiny scarlet roots find their way. And so must we.

Reconnecting with Papatūānuku is the focus for us today, and that reconnection means reclaiming our healthy identity as those who are inseparable from her. We are part of her and she of us.

Walking in those footsteps of old, feeling our tūpuna stamping their original haka. Being in places that have meaning and history for us. The childhood beaches, those first fishing trips, standing on our maunga, our mountains, being with our whānau as the evening's embers die down. Hearing those stories over again, like the well-thumbed pages of ancient texts. Where we are from. These are the lands, places, valleys and coves that not only shaped us, they are us, and we are them.

Remembering brings with it tears. That aroha we share with the whenua spills out of our eyes. We feel it in our gut, in our hearts. In our sobs.

The activity on this Oike moon prepares us for three days of a different kind of reflection. Let that energy drain away, and with it, the last remnants of the desire to control Papatūānuku. Feel it as sweat dripping from your skin, as today's haka comes to an end.

'Ko te maumahara kore ki ngā whakapapa o ōu mātua tūpuna, e rite ana ki te pūkaki awa kāore ōna hikuawa, ki te rākau rānei kāore ōna pakiaka.' As Te Wharehuia Milroy said, if you cannot recall the genealogy of your ancestors, you are like a brook without a source, a tree without roots. Know where you come from.

Make Oike our day to recover this mātauranga, this wisdom, to the centre of our healthy collective identity. How can we begin to create restorative wawata, healing dreams for reclaiming our ūkaipō relationship with mother earth right here and now, and with each Oike from here on? Learning the places and practices of old, always considering the reciprocity between our precious ūkaipō and ourselves. Maintaining a close scrutiny of defences we might use to condone any ongoing abuse of Papatūānuku. What does she say to you when you work to restore your relationship? Are you listening?

Korekore

Moving up the generational chain

He aha te mea nui o te ao? He tāngata, he tāngata, he tāngata.

What is the most important thing in the world? It is people, it is people, it is people.

Each stage has its lessons.

The first night of the Korekore moons, a time for honouring our losses.

I am returned to stories of my own people and of our wāhine.

Meri Ngāroto of Te Aupōuri was married to Puhipi Te Ripi, chief of Te Rarawa, one of several arranged marriages between our iwi. The old people completed a ritual to ensure they had no offspring. In her grief she composed the famous saying:

‘Hūtia te rito o te harakeke, kei hea te kōmako e kō?

Māu e ui mai, he aha te mea nui o te ao?

Māku e kī atu, he tāngata, he tāngata, he tāngata.’

If you remove the heart of the flax bush, from where will the bellbird sing?

If you say to me, what is the most important thing in this world? My reponse is, it is people, it is people, it is people.

The anguish of her words. Realising she would never bear a child.

From our ūkaipō dreaming insights last night our thoughts expand. Our generational gears are shifting.

This is the moon that takes me back to when it hit me that I could no longer get pregnant and have children. It was 2020 and I had begun a new relationship. He was younger than me, with no children. At first I was very clear. I do not want to have more kids, I am too old.

That was our understanding. Then I found myself thinking about it differently — maybe, just maybe. The seed of the idea began to take hold. I thought about getting pregnant again and having more children. I know, right, what was going on, what the hell was I thinking? You are not as shocked as I was to be thinking about this at 54 years of age. What?

I felt physically strong and full of energy. And so loved, adored in a way I had not experienced before. I still had my awa. My whare tangata, my womb, was still bringing her sacred tides. My body felt young.

Maybe it was an ancient evolutionary drive to want to create a baby in that state. High on oxytocin. High on love and desire. And perhaps as an antidote to the pandemic horror around us.

I really wanted us to have tamariki, to have children together. Not for me alone. For my partner, for us as a couple, as a whānau. I felt I needed to be able to give that to him. Anything less felt like I wasn't doing my part. And beneath that feeling, there was a sense that without that I wasn't enough. If I couldn't do that for us, for our whakapapa, lineage, then what use was I? I saw the next shared generation as a meaningful way to join our whānau together forever. That was the dream, the fantasy for a while.

It was Korekore, te tuatahi, the first Korekore moon when I finally realised I was deluding myself. This was my ngeri, my own short inward haka. Dropping the protective emotional shield, and finally facing up to my own inner demons with a raw heart.

Hina's shadows delivered the final gut punch realisation. I would never have another baby.

I would never breastfeed again, wake in the night to the tiny cries and soothe a little one in my arms in the same way. I would never experience that again, as I had with my two precious, and now adult, babies.

I was unprepared for the hard cold grief that washed over me at first. The dark shadow of this first Korekore smacked my face. Salt in the eyes. The stinging tears. What did it mean about me as a woman now that I could no longer bring forth babies? I had not realised this was such a fundamental part of my identity. Most of my life I had been taking my fertility for granted. I had been fortunate to conceive when I chose to.

This night of Hina's light and shade helped me to figure out this was the right time for my own private letting go. That freedom, realising I can be in the relationship as just me. I was enough. We are enough.

Korekore is always a deep thinking time for me. The first of these moody days, the contrasting dark shadow moving steadily across Hina's light face. And I always take a moment to reflect on my movement up into the next stage of my life at this time of the month. The ruminations about the end of the fertile identity, the treasured core of me for most of my life are farewelled with a warm lingering hug. The idea of my own worth as so intimately tied to my ability to have a pēpi, a baby, loosening in my mind. Relaxing into wawata, dreams of this Korekore light's embrace.

In our culture the status of older women can be such a positive one. In this Korekore moon I stop to pay homage, to think about my senior female relations and colleagues. All of their sacrifices. All of their contrasts, their subdued and their loud support. Their encouragement, their challenge, their expectations, their wawata. I sense the dreams they have for us, their descendants, and for the generations to come. I take the dream baton as they hand it forward. I recognise my place in the whakapapa, in the descent lines, a relay of women's dreaming.

By the light of our Korekore moon find the stillness within our own pā harakeke, our own families. The courage to catch the dreams passed on by those women willing you on.

You are part of that long line, moving up the generational chain, living our dreams since time immemorial and passing them on again and again, over the horizon.

Korekore tuarua

Our personal health

Te tū wāhine.

Female stance.

Standing in our own health.

Hinenuitepō, goddess of the underworld, was having a well earned nap. She has to take her rest too. Māui-tikitiki-a-Taranga, Māui for short, the well-known demigod, the trickster, had what he thought was a great idea. He decided to seek immortality by attempting to reverse the birthing process. His strategy was that if he entered Hinenuitepō's iho rangi, her vagina, and travelled backwards up to the whare tangata, her womb, he could ensure immortality for humans. Quite a plan.

Māui was the original shapeshifter. He had turned himself into many creatures before. This time he morphed himself into a tuatara. A creature he felt was fit for the task, for the journey inside the goddess. A pīwaiwaka, a fantail, saw this and started laughing. You have to admit, it must have looked pretty ridiculous. The chuckling woke the goddess. She immediately spotted what was going on and crushed Māui to death with her pelvic floor muscles.

Among the many lessons of this time-honoured pūrākau, this ancient story, one that stands out for me is the mana, the status and respect our culture has for the strength of that part of our female bodies. Not to be messed with. The importance of dangerously healthy pelvic floor muscles.

A few years back, I became involved in some research investigating a sensor worn inside the vagina, to help us wāhine, us women, learn to use our pelvic floor muscles more effectively to guard against urinary incontinence. My mind immediately returned to our venerable description of Hinenuitepō and her deadly pelvic floor. We all know about the exercises we can do to strengthen our pelvic floor muscles, right? But it turns out the way most of us do the exercises isn't getting the job done. And we pay the price! Sex can hurt, we worry about 'accidents', and the smell, we stop going out, we wear multiple pairs of undies, it can all get pretty overwhelming and very, very sad.

I wanted to make sure that our stories as Māori women were heard and taken seriously in informing the development of this device.

A group of us wāhine held a wānanga, a forum at the marae, to talk about our experiences as part of the project. We had a chance to try out the prototype device, too. As you can imagine, there was plenty of laughter, even though we were talking about such a heavy subject. And of course the issue of improved sexual pleasure with use of the device was discussed. So much fun getting together as wāhine. Talking about serious, often painful experiences, and yet we were never far from the humorous side of things.

Our tūpuna, our forebears, were familiar with using implements inserted into te iho rangi, the vagina. Some were used when women were alone in childbirth. Certain types of moss were also used internally during menstruation.

Our Korekore tuarua, our Korekore rawea moon as she is also known, is a time when nature is closing up. It is the time I reflect on the specific challenges our bodies have and the ripple effect on our relationships with ourselves and others.

Let this second of our Korekore moons provide you with time to free up your wawata, your dreams, and plan for your own intimate health. Whether or not you have a whare tangata, a womb, the pelvic floor musculature is vital for holding up your internal organs. Channel even just a tiny, mortal amount of the immense power of Hinenuitepō and her pelvic floor haka, and feel all the life-affirming benefits.

Korekore piri ki Tangaroa

New ways to move forward

Ka pū te ruha ka hao te rangatahi.

The old net is cast aside.

Old approaches must make way for new.

Our COVID experiences have certainly forced us to take this thinking to a whole new level.

The old life, our old familiar routines have changed forever. We have had to adapt in so many ways.

The wisdom of our whakataukī and whakatauākī, our proverbs, have been helpful during this ongoing evolving disaster of global proportions.

There has been no one single COVID experience. There is so much variation. So many different shades of grief, ambiguous loss, alongside very tangible losses and pain. And we humans are simply not designed for the loss of connection, and disruption of routines and expectations. Our magical thinking ripped away.

We feel the impact in every aspect of our being.

And today is a very fitting day to reflect on the pandemic effect of our era.

Today is the last of our three Korekore moons. Korekore piri ki Tangaroa.

Over the last two days of Korekore moons we have remembered our losses, we have embraced where we are in life. The generational shifts we feel as we age. The impact on our most intimate physical and emotional health. Where we fit in our whakapapa, our descent lines.

We have paid homage at the house of Hinenuitepō, goddess of the underworld, for another month. And now the waves begin to build again. And before the Tangaroa moons, we have this day.

Korekore piri, the moon closest to Tangaroa, god of the sea. A unique time and place.

Because time and place are not so distinct in our world. Wā, time and wāhi place, even the words indicate an intimate connection, a clear bond. The intersection of time and place.

We describe opportunity in te reo Māori, in the Māori language, as 'whai wāhi'. We might translate that as the seeking of place and time. That time and place occurring together to create freedom. An opening up of their woven natures, for something new to happen. Korekore piri ki Tangaroa has its own special time and place for us. Right now, right here.

The moon has such a unique role in how we experience time and place. She holds both sacred and practical realms in her gaze. Our tūpuna, our ancestors, lived their daily lives according to the depth of their wisdom about the moon's influence. They needed that in order to survive. They knew about the moon as part of the whānau mārama, the extended family of celestial beings. And they recognised her intimate relationship with Tangaroa and Hinemoana, the deities of the oceans. They felt Hina's pull on those mighty forces in creating tides. And especially her hold on the emotional tides of human beings.

Our emotions, the workings of our minds —
they are governed by our own female goddess.
Hinengaro is our female deity of the mind. She is
in my mind a lot. She is my mind.

And after all, I am a psychiatrist. For me
Hinengaro is at the centre of what I try to do in
my work every day. To understand her workings
for different whānau and discover together what
she is up to. And I wonder why she is called
Hinengaro. Ngaro is a word that can be translated
as many things: to be hidden, to be absent, to
be missing or lost, to be consumed, to pass into
something, to go unnoticed, to subside, to be
forgotten, to be unintelligible, to be baffled, to be
distressed, oppressed, overcome, to be unrequited,
to be certain, to do something secretly. I imagine
Hinengaro in her marae, the marae of the mind.
Multi-tasking as we wāhine, as we women often
do. I imagine her karanga, her call to the other
female deities, welcoming them to her whare,
her abode. Her waiata, her songs, sublime and
compelling, unlocking tears of recognition and
waves of remembrance. Her laughter, her secrets
and her fascinations. I see her flying across time
and space, the past, future and right now.

So here we are in a pandemic. And we are learning about life with COVID variants.

We have rediscovered our sense of being a global whānau, a worldwide family. Whānau members dying in different parts of the world from COVID have set in motion intergenerational waves of grief and loss. Parents behaving in ways never seen before by their whānau. Tamariki, mokopuna, children and grandchildren in fear and shock.

How do we learn to take care of ourselves and those we care about, those who live close by? We have had to really reflect on what it means to be under stress, haven't we? How are we going with that? We are tired, not sleeping well, we are more likely to make poor decisions, be irritable and distracted. How are we owning that? And how do we learn from the flow-on effects? How do we discuss this openly, and is that safe for us in the different places we work and live? How might we lead by example and make those conversations normal.

This last Korekore moon is that critical time to reflect with our precious Hinengaro, our female goddess of the mind. To acknowledge her need to roam free. Her haka, her dance of challenge, untethered. We have a new imperative, a new reason to really change. This pandemic gives us reasons. To discover what it means to have this extraordinary creative mind and to garner our skills for the better. How to release our wawata, our dreams, for our own mind's sake, to let go of attempts to control Hinengaro. To embrace her hidden places, her uncertainty. She has so much stored up for us. We must find that new net she has made to catch meaningful, healthy ways to be. Hinengaro has such a wealth of resources and aroha. Feel her hurl that new net from the depths of her void as she performs her own haka welcoming Tangaroa's vibrant waves this month.

Let's examine the haul. What treasures does Hinengaro's rangatahi, her fishing net of new thinking bring forward this Korekore piri ki Tangaroa?

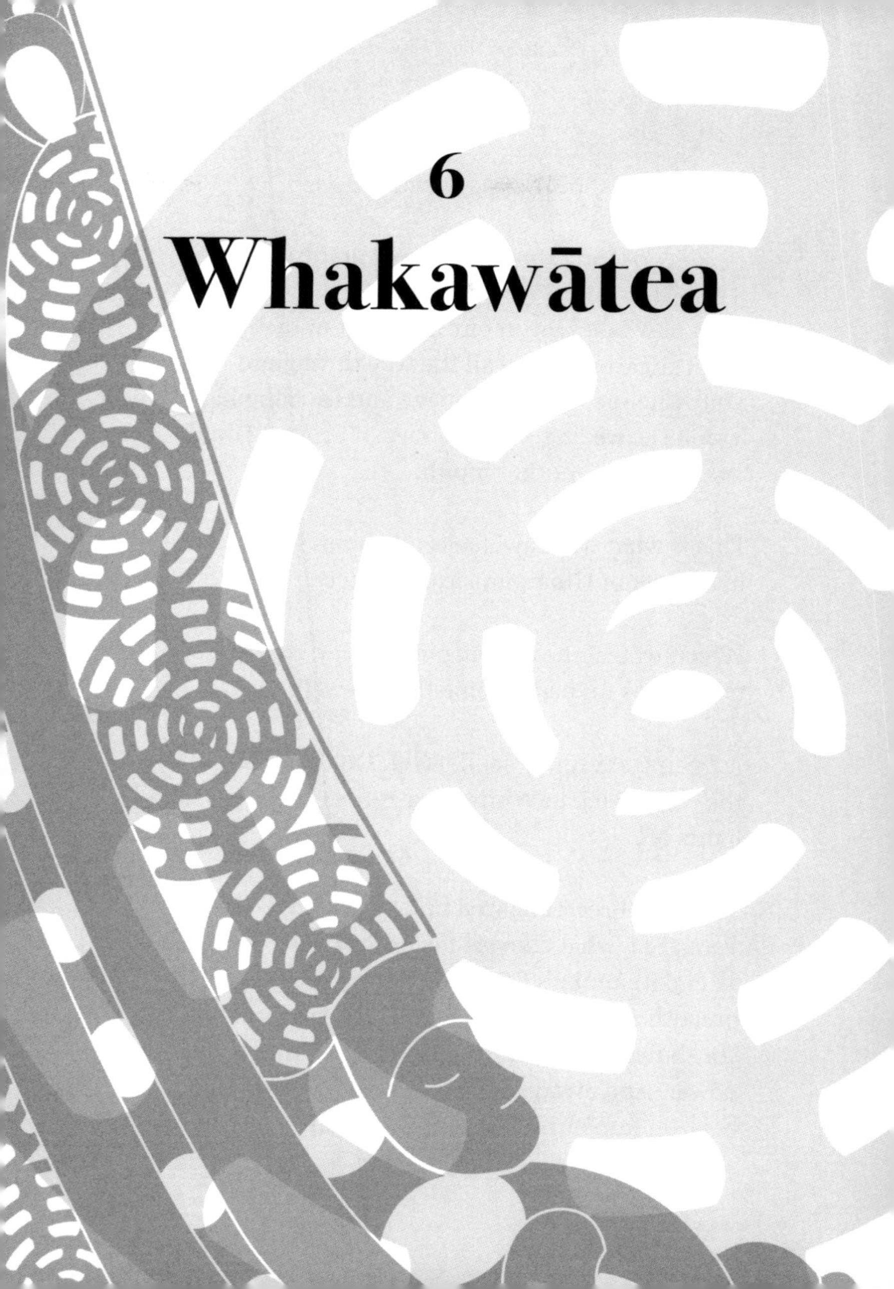

6
Whakawātea

Mihi whakamutunga.

A long slow offering of gratitude.

Hina now takes us on our final part of the journey. Our Tangaroa moons all the way through to Mutuwhenua. Paying homage and learning big lessons as we linger on our circuit around Hina's teachings for another month.

This is what whakawātea is all about. Here we are, in the last of Hina's musical brackets.

Whakawātea, the clearing of the way. A series of tributes as we bring home the farewell.

A freeing energy to send us off. Our completion of the circle back to Whiro. Our return to the reset and lights off.

The first three Tangaroa moons are high octane. Tangaroa, what a lover! For some iwi he is regarded as Papatūānuku's first love. Before Ranginui. His breadth and depth, and width. His rhythm, his vocabulary of touch. He has it all. All that water power. And always with that reach beyond the horizon into our futures. Our Tangaroa moons also have some very specific celestial responsibilities. These are the moons signalling the time to celebrate Matariki, Māori new year, in midwinter.

Tāne is next. He opened up our world, bringing in Te Ao Mārama, the world of light. He is our overachiever. With so many faces and roles. The bringer of the baskets of knowledge, father of the birds, god of the forests and progenitor of humankind.

Rongo, our deity of peace and calm. God of the garden. As we pass through his gaze we grow, we shift, maybe almost imperceptibly. He draws us in to observe, yes, we are changing. The endurance of Rongo for us as women, the discovery of intergenerational healing, this is the call.

Maurea is the name we use in Te Hiku, also known as Mauri, for Hina's penultimate face. Our essence. Our priorities.

We are here for our monthly overhaul, this is the right time for the work to get done.

Finally, and how fitting. Mutuwhenua. Completion. The land of our travels is closing up. Hina's whenua, the land beneath her, is almost invisible again.

This whakawātea is the final stage in our Hina journey home, our kete wawata, our baskets of dreams, being filled with new insights from these distinguished deities.

We cannot stop to get off this lunar tour, even if we wanted to. Are you ready? That's us.

Tangaroa ā-mua

Laughter as medicine

Mātiro whakamua.

Look beyond the horizon. Beyond the obvious.

Use the power of laughter to dream your future.

Tangaroa god of the sea, beyond the horizon. Our tūpuna, our forebears, are very specific about the way in which we start with Tangaroa. Reconnecting with this vast unquenchable Tangaroa vitality and endurance.

Tangaroa ā-mua (not 'ō mua', not in the past).

Hina's face today is very much about the future. Tangaroa of the future, this is how we begin our four Tangaroa days and nights. Mātiro whakamua, to look beyond the horizon. Hina begins to rise after midnight and sets closer and closer to midday. Our Tangaroa moons are very present in our mornings.

The invitation of Hina's Tangaroa ā-mua is to envision the future. To dream our futures into life.

We have a saying about that, too, 'Ka mua ka muri' looking back in order to go forward.

Or, for some, 'Kia whakatōmuri te haere whakamua' walking backwards into the future.

Our tūpuna reminding us to hold on to past learnings, to hold on to their legacy, to inform our future.

So I travel back in my mind. It was 1985 when I first experienced the vast expanse of Tangaroa. I was on a Danish cargo ship laden with apples bound for Hong Kong. I had been working as a waitress in Tāmaki Makaurau, in Auckland. One of my friends was the sous-chef. Her father was a shipping agent. And so we were lucky enough to have the chance to travel on board to Hong Kong. Our quarters were the medical clinic, an intriguing omen of my future. From there the plan was meeting up with some friends who were studying in Beijing. Such were the relative travel freedoms of that era.

The ship's crew were a mix of people from all over

the world, men and women. Engineers, chefs, a maintenance team, and of course, the captain. The Danish hospitality was exceptional. And the fun. We played Danish bingo most nights, and learned a few Danish phrases along the way, especially the ones that are so hard to pronounce. 'Rødgrød med fløde', a kind of red porridge with cream. And a pretty challenging phrase, classic for providing Danes with hours of fun at the foreigners' expense.

I can picture the first time we were in the middle of the ocean with no land in sight anywhere, the water stretching away in every direction. I was startled. I couldn't quite believe it. No land at all. I turned around several times to check. No, no land. Only waves, peaks and troughs, dark grey as far as the eye could see. And what a completely new reference point. Such a contrast from being in a plane. Somehow being above the clouds when over the ocean hadn't got to me in the same way. I remember my mind racing, flooded with thoughts about escape, nowhere to run to get away from this endless ocean. There was an intensity that just hit me. Looking out across these undulating watery plains I suddenly felt so alive, so much more aware of everything around me. And I was a bit scared, it was unfamiliar, it was just so big. I thought about the crew and how this was the norm for them, and if they could cope with it, and learn to enjoy and have fun in this extraordinary watery world, then so could I.

Those memories of being in the middle of the ocean will never leave me. Getting my balance on board, in every way. The huge waves rolling the massive ship, rolling me in my bed. Holding on to the rail. Feeling the power of Tangaroa on this massive vessel. All of us held in Tangaroa's sway.

And, we are all re-learning to find our balance, in life.

How can we feel okay with even exploring balance that includes having fun and pleasure in our lives when so much of the world is gripped by war, the ravages of pandemic and climate emergency? How do we bring the Tangaroa ā-mua, that future ocean legacy into our daily lives? Because believing in that view beyond the horizon is ultimately about hope. And hope seems a bit unrealistic right now.

It is not easy. I imagine a slow-motion version of my adjustment on board that container ship in 1985. It has felt like that moving back into lockdowns with this latest strain of COVID. And recognising there will be more strains, more restrictions. That this is part of the Tangaroa we must factor into our future thinking.

These big ocean rollers, out in Tangaroa. Tangaroa thumping the sides of our waka, our ship. And the waka, the vessel of the mind, body, wairua, and all our relationships, reminds us of the power of the elements in our world. Keeps us humble. I suppose that is where I find myself. Starting small.

We can have complex plans with lots of words, and they can be very helpful, don't get me wrong. And, when we are all running on empty, with chronic stress response and compassion fatigue, what can we cling to?

When we were on board that container ship we made sure to laugh a lot. I was a passenger, an observer for much of the trip, and the crew included me. And we had strong enough ties to relax and have fun. To laugh and enjoy our camaraderie on board. To learn from each other's resilience.

This is the legacy for today. We don't have all the answers. There is no paint-by-numbers solution.

And yet we can find an energy and even a joy in recognising that Tangaroa will always be there in our futures.

Have you ever been out in the open sea? How did it feel? Maybe life feels like that at the moment, without the usual reference points. We have lived through such confinement, all in our little waka bubbles, a skill set we have learned to keep at the ready. How to build a sense of fun in the context of such gloom?

I think about the people I laugh with. I return to my young laughter as a kōtiro, a girl. Laughing until I cried with my female friends at school. We would laugh so much together. Every single day. I am trying to remember when that daily experience stopped. Maybe starting university? Somewhere in there life got serious and that freedom to laugh openly was set aside.

I laugh so much with my kids these days. Through the recent lockdown my daughter Millie and I were in our own bubble with the three dogs. Hangareka, she's a natural comic and we so easily make each other laugh until we cry. She reminds me so much of Mum and I see her face in pictures of my nan.

We are women who can laugh. Must laugh. Mum, me and Millie, Nan. Especially at ourselves. And I go back to Nan again, Mum's mother, who I never knew.

She died when Mum was pregnant with me. Her face clearly our faces too. I imagine her laughing with us, Annie Yates. Our tiny part of this whakapapa, this descent line that reaches into the future of my wawata, my dreams, on this Tangaroa ā-mua moon. My wawata filled with the collective squeals of joy that our descendants will have, whatever the troubles in their time, and somehow they will hear us, our laughter caught on the sea spray.

When was a time in life you laughed, really laughed, until it hurt, until you cried? Especially when life felt so out of control, so painful?

Today is the day to kick-start Tangaroa moons with laughter.

Tangaroa ā-roto

Inner emotional travel

Tangaroa whakamau tai.

Tangaroa commander of the waves.

Tangaroa, solace in uncertainty.

Let's paddle out into the magical night of Tangaroa ā-roto, and then return with renewed vigour as the waves fill us with their encouragement.

Tangaroa, our ocean deity, governs several nights of our lunar cycle. A time of energy, of collective action, of getting out of the house. Replenishing ourselves and restoring our wairua, our souls. It's a time to set things in motion. Time to make things happen.

So, are you ready? Have you got our hoe? Our paddles?

This is the karakia we say before we go out paddling.

Whakataka te hau ki te uru.

Whakataka te hau ki te tonga.

Kia mākinakina ki uta.

Kia mātaratara ki tai.

E hī ake ana te atakura.

He tio, he huka, he hauhunga.

Tihei mauri ora.

The west wind has shifted and the south wind has dropped.

The land bristles, and the sea has goosebumps.

The first rays of a red dawn pierce the night,

Revealing snow, ice and frost from the mountains to the sea.

I bind myself to this.*

* Translation by Judge Sir Joseph Williams, KNZM, Ngāti Pūkenga, Waitaha, Tapuika.

We are going for a paddle together tonight. Our rhythm; in together, out together, reminds us of the rhythms of our own ocean, inside. Our own salty inner oasis. Tangaroa ā-roto, meaning within our own intimate Tangaroa. How do we feel in these times of fluctuating confinement, isolation now so much more familiar? Those inner tides, our breakers, our rips and currents. Where thoughts and feelings surf through us in these times of oscillating levels of uncertainty. Where sometimes, we feel pulled under by that inner whirlpool.

There are so many kupu Māori, words for uncertainty because uncertainty is not new to us. Our ancestors knew how to convey the various shades of uncertainty across time, their knowing embedded in our reo, our language, ready for our tongues to unwrap.

Rangirua, to be in doubt, to be uncertain. Literally two rangi, two different skies, two differing outlooks. Ngākaurua, uncertain, ambivalent, being pulled in two heartfelt directions. Then there is pōnānātanga, confusion, uncertainty. Pō, night, and nānā to tend carefully, to nurse. So pō indicating that the ability to care for and nurture is housed in darkness, is not accessible. And pōkaikaha, confused, at a loss, flustered, baffled, bamboozled. Again, the word pō for night, combined with kaikaha, the word for eagerness, showing how that eagerness is shrouded in darkess, unavailable.

So much talk of uncertainty in these times, as if it is novel, when really, we know it so well. Uncertainty, our old friend and companion. And yet there is a new flavour of uncertainty with us now. As a Māori psychiatrist I feel it in my daily work. Listening intently to our young people and those who care for them. I am witnessing a new generation of a shadowy old face, forming as it rises up higher and higher, demanding recognition, rising up like the tide. At this Tangaroa-ā-roto, our inner neap tide grinds away, insistent in its reminder. The steady pull of submerged waves within us. We must match these tides with the consistent strokes of our inner emotional paddling. We must keep our rhythm, despite our wildly fluctuating, at times out of control, stress levels.

Pandemic. Millions of people around the world have already passed on. Here in Aotearoa we have been so deeply affected in our own unique ways. The grief of not being able to attend tangihanga, funerals, for months, of not being able to hongi, to share breath.

And the global anguish of touch being something to fear.

Not knowing how long we can hold on in our isolation and loneliness. And the ambiguous losses, when it is not so clear what has been lost. Dread of our uncertain future. Feeling fragile as the rules keep changing, with no solid ground to stand on.

In the Starship regional inpatient mental health unit for children and teenagers with serious mental ill health we could not have visitors in the usual way. Restricted visitor numbers were down to one during lockdowns, our most highly constrained times. The pain and suffering of separation. Loss of not being there on the journey with loved ones. Losing time, days rolling together in an eerie kind of groundhog day. The whānau, family members, hobbling along in a strange emotional three-legged race to get through each day. Feeling something is gone but not being able to put your finger on it. Ambiguity defying resolution.

The last two years of rolling lockdowns have been so hard. I am often tired, irritable, feeling helpless and ineffective, lonely and then, paradoxically wanting to isolate more. Why do I feel angry and sceptical? Guilty for having seemingly few impacts but devastated inside, a kind of survivor guilt and shame. All mixed in with what was already going on, feeling close to the edge, overworked, all our previous vulnerabilities somehow more raw.

Who will live and who will die?

What I see each day in my job is people who are increasingly desperate. The new uncertainties compounding the struggle to find reasons to live. People craving and rejecting closeness at the same time. People turning themselves into robots to cope, shutting down their need for connection as a coping strategy, only to find it impossible to open those channels again when it is safer. The lingering effects those slow persistent waves that creep up the beach of our minds rubbing away the messages we left to ourselves in the sand. Tide after tide of uncertainty, of living in limbo, breaking down the most resilient among us. This is the other side of the pandemic. For those who survive, the cruel storms of the COVID sea washing away our ability to be connected. Not so great for the immune system, either.

And yet here we are on our waka, our ocean-going vessel, paddling as best we can, both inside and out.

Our tikanga, our practices, strengthening our ability to manage the uncertainty, moving with it, paddling alongside it. Tikanga, returning our minds and our hearts to those aspects that anchor us in land, sky and sea. We are our oceans, our land, our sky. When we tune in to what is already around us this gives us some sense of certainty.

And we have the power of telling our stories. These are the stories that never get old.

These are the ones that continue to resonate as they carry the power of naming. Naming uncertainty in its new guise. Talking about how it tries to weasel its way into our minds and set up base there, unchecked. Reminding ourselves life has always been uncertain and closure is a myth. We like to pretend that life is more sure, when really that just isn't true.

And there is always eye contact, those watery lenses into the soul. Truly seeing each other and ourselves. Masked and unmasked. See those tears, see that fear, that pain, that suffering. Sharing our uncertainty without words, being prepared to let others see those turbulent inner waves, that is a true source of comfort.

And as we turn our waka for home, ka haere te waka ki uta, our wawata, our dreams, coming in to the shore. Feel the surety of the sand holding our feet.

We have always lived with uncertainty. And we are never alone. We have our own Tangaroa ā-roto wherever our waka takes us. Lighting those inner emotional travels, buoying us up. Facing our own stories of uncertainty. Resisting the desire to cover up, and conceal what we are processing from ourselves. Today is for trusting our inner ocean tides.

Tangaroa ata kiokio

Longing

Māu anō te tinana, māku te ata o te tāpara kau atu e.

For you the physical reality, for me merely the shadow of desire.

Loneliness and longing for our loved ones.

Tangaroa ata kiokio, also known as Tangaroa whāriki kiokio.

A morning carpet of kiokio, the palm-leaf fern. Tangaroa in the form of kiokio.

Kiokio is the name for the dense covering of the pinky-red shaded fern that envelops the riverbanks, the undergrowth of the bush.

Have you seen it? The kiokio hugging into Papatūānuku. Folding like a rich velvet cloak.

Hugging her curves. The flush of pink, like the skin on your neck blushing with pleasure.

Tangaroa, our ocean covered with shot silk is our twilight tonight. At both ends of the day, these are our colours.

We see such spectacular peach gloamings from this promontory of Te Motu Ārai Roa, Waiheke Island. Looking out from the bay, separated from our loved ones. The rippling coral and verdigris patina leading all the way back to Tāmaki Makaurau, to Auckland.

Tāmaki of a hundred lovers. Such a potent symbol of loneliness. So near and yet so far.

How does a place named for love and connection cope with such confinement? Even our land, our whenua in her kiokio sheath grieves.

The rolling waves singing our whakawātea, our closing song, across Tīkapa Moana, the Hauraki Gulf. This whāriki, this woven mat of kiokio calling to us. A song of memories lying on that bed of pliant soft ferns. Memories of kisses and the softest strokes of skin on skin.

A salutation to the opening of food wrapped in our kiokio, cooked in hāngi, in the earth oven. Eating the succulent fronds. Such a sensual time. This last crescent of Tangaroa holding all of Hina's shadow in his jewelled hands.

In Tangaroa, our whāriki of kiokio spills over into all of our spaces. The ferns creating dappled soft light, cascading into our lives to end this last of Tangaroa's moons.

Painful reminders of times past. Intimacy that will never be quite the same again.

How do we let ourselves submerge into the sumptuous plush folds of Tangaroa's waves today for comfort? The colours of Papatūānuku's clothing resonating with Tangaroa's cloak. Melding together as they did many years ago. For some, they were the original lovers.

Earth mother and sea. They draw us back under their blanket of reminiscence. Together and yet separated. Much like our lives, marked from here on in by degrees of isolation.

Tangaroa ata kiokio might be a private, self-loving

time for you. As you sit with these yearning feelings. You might need to connect with a lover or friend. What soothing wawata, what dreams can you conjure up this Tangaroa moon, swimming across the waves at twilight? The rouge-tinged light shining in our eyes. Loneliness softened.

Ōtāne

Finding our space

Kia whakarongo rua rā ō tātou taringa ki te waha o Tāne.

Let's listen to the birds.

Tāne has a lot to say today.

Tāne is the kid who pushed his parents apart.

Literally. He lay down on his mother, Papatūānuku, pushed up with his legs against Ranginui, sky father, and prised them away from each other. Not everyone was happy about this. Ranginui and Papatūānuku mourned their loss of intimacy. Other tamariki, other children, were beside themselves. Whānau life, even for deities, was not all plain sailing. Our Māori cosmology teaches some tough lessons about being whānau.

Tāne, for some, he is the mātāmua, the eldest, he

is the one who took the drastic and decisive action. He wasn't trying to end their relationship. He was responding to the cramped, dark conditions that the whānau of our atua, our deities, were living in. By separating the tight embrace of his parents he created space and light. We call this Te Ao Mārama, The World of Light. The world of enlightenment. Tāne made it happen.

We experience similar things as mere mortals too. Children's arrival in our lives means there needs to be more space in adult relationships. Pregnancy is a time when the reality of what is coming begins to dawn on parents and caregivers. And then delivery makes this irrefutable. Adjustments must be made. No one can fully prepare you for this realisation, that there needs to be more elbow room. Not only physical space, either. Heart space needs to open up too. Emotional space which shifts and flows over the years as needs change and develop, and as the life cycle of the whānau shifts. Anyone who has brought up kids can relate to the Tāne effect. Feeling prised away from how things were before.

And as kids ourselves we have all had time in Tāne's shoes, haven't we? We have layers of feelings, ways of knowing, memories about our own effect of coming into the world and our experiences of the space and light we created.

The pandemic has really complicated whānau experiences of room to move, light and dark, knowledge and awareness, hasn't it? Especially with the lack of space, being forced into such close range to each other. And at the same time being restricted from other places we can safely go. We are not used to this confinement. It gives us a new perspective on how Papatūānuku and Ranginui, with their more than 70 progeny, felt. A sense of being trapped. It has made me appreciate Tāne in a whole new way. So many families have been stuck together. Kids seeing so much more of their parents than ever before. Living cheek by jowl, former private times a thing of the past. And over such long periods. Some of this has been incredible, whānau forced together like the proverbial sardines in a can. Discovering who we are in this age of fear and uncertainty, and finding strength in those discoveries. For some, becoming closer has meant a profound sense of appreciation. And for others it has exposed a deep sense of helplessness and defeat.

In my daily work I have seen the absolute helplessness of parents and caregivers. I have seen a very real erosion of parents' and caregivers' confidence, of their sense of what to do after the pandemic hit. Standing as parents in a whole new way. How have we navigated the closure of schools, loss of routines, bedtimes, mealtimes and outings? Managing relationships with whānau inside and outside of the bubbles we have lived in. How to find any of our own emotional space? And the anger, rage, fear experienced by our tamariki of all ages. Development regressing, learning stalling, a locking down, an emotional freezing. Constantly playing catch up to what our whānau needs are now. And always the fear in the back of our minds, anticipating the worst.

The world we live in now is strangely similar to the one our parents and older generations grew up in. Just going back a few generations. From my greats, to my grandparents, to my parents, to what I have tried to do as a mother. My mind boggles. I have learned a new respect for my forebears. We have all struggled with how each generation tested the limits. Tested patience. Tested what it means to be in a parenting role and the relationship with our young ones. And we have a new gratitude to our forebears for their lives and their deaths through pandemics in their time.

Hina shows us how to pay homage to Tāne. Ō Tāne, about Tāne, of Tāne. You are very familiar with this aspect of our reo, Māori language grammar by now. Tāne gives us so much to draw on today. After his actions to create light and space for his whānau to thrive, he went on to gift us the resources to power our hearts and our wawata, our dreams. He was by all accounts a bit of an overachiever. Tāne is the one who brought us the three baskets of knowledge, by the power of his mind.

'Kotahi tonu te hiringa i kake ai a Tāne ki Tikitiki-o-Rangi, ko te hiringa i te mahara.'

There was but one power that enabled Tāne to ascend to the uppermost heavens, it was the power of the mind.

'Ngā kete o te wānanga, ko te kete tuauri, ko te kete tuatea, ko te kete aronui.'

The three baskets of learning and knowledge, and their specific names.

These refrains come from a famous song about Tāne's exploits.

Te kete tuauri contained sacred learning of rites and customs, our tikanga. Our wawata, our dreams and aspirations came with te kete tuauri.

Te kete tuatea contained the deep dark magic, alongside evil and war. As well as agricultural know-how, and proficiency in working with stone and earth.

Finally, te kete aronui, containing philosophies and wisdom to promote advancement of wellbeing, relationships, aroha, creative expression and arts.

One of Tāne's challenges for us today is how to put into practice the baskets of knowledge we were handed from our parents, from our caregivers, that are now in our hands.

Noticing how our perspective changes when we can look back on what they went through.

This world of light and learning carries with it responsibilities and challenges too. The push and pull of this Ōtāne moon. The sway of the trees, the signature flutter of birds' wings and the lilt of their calls.

This Ōtāne, our wawata can be about how tamariki, how children naturally create light and space in our lives. And we are all tamariki, aren't we? How can you bring some more light and room to move emotionally into your own life today? How much more of Te Ao Mārama can you let in on this Ōtāne?

Ōrongonui

Intergenerational peace

Rongo-ā-whare.

Peace brought about by women.

Where does your source of peace reside?

Ōrongonui, a time for sensations. For our senses. Hearing, smelling, tasting, listening, touching. Our gut feelings. This is Rongo time.

Rongo is his nickname. More formally known as Rongomātāne, the deity of peace and fertility. The energy of the whare hui, inside the meeting house, where his oversight provides the safety for robust debate and discussion, all held in his peaceful gaze. Mr Chill. But don't get me wrong. His korowai, his cloaking of our discussions doesn't mean they are in any way muted or less vigorous. Far from it. His mandate means that verbal tussling can safely get really heated.

Ōrongonui signals this intense feeling time. A garden of feeling plants erupts up from fertile soil. Just like plants after some sun and rain, suddenly they sprout overnight. This is the power of Rongo. He is king of the garden and of ripe fecundity. The kūmara deity.

We also talk about Rongo-ā-whare, peace brought about by the mediation of women.

The whare being a metaphor for us women, as the whare tangata, houses of people.

This is the day each month when I choose to quite deliberately think about my own whare tangata, my womb. If she had her own voice, what does she need me to listen to today? How does she call to me? What is she trying to tell me?

I hark back to when I had a procedure to explore why I was having unusually heavy uterine bleeding. I watched on the monitor as inner undulating peaks and valleys, like the sand dunes up home in the Far North, came into view. These needed to be cut back. Scraped down. And despite everyone's best efforts this was excruciatingly painful.

Luckily my daughter was with me. Gripping her hand and looking into her eyes gave me such strength. She brought me into her own Rongo-ā-whare, her own serenity. She gave generously of her intergenerational medicine. My daughter was nurtured in this very place. My whare tangata, my womb. Mother to daughter, daughter to mother.

I am reminded how lucky I have been in my relationship with my whare tangata. She has carried my pēpi, my babies. Her own delicate senses so attuned to holding them safe. Her karanga, her call continuing to connect us all. Through time's threads. Weaving and spiritually linking future and past generations. Ancient and uplifting through those times.

Now she calls to connect me to our generations of women at a different time of life. It felt so right that my daughter was there to hand me over to them, to this rōpū of wāhine, this next generation of women. Handing me gently over into the next chapter of life. This time where we no longer carry pēpi in our whare tangata, in our wombs. My whare has sung of her aging pains alright. And yet her moonlit whakawātea, her closing song, has a new lightness and freedom. I feel so contented and safe that she and I still travel together. The pleasure we have had together in life, alongside the pain.

How can you use this time to open up wawata that Ōrongonui has to offer you about your body, your māra, your life's garden, no matter what stage of life you are in? How can you focus in on your sense of peace, that silken thread of our intergenerational healing?

Maurea/Mauri

Perspective

He maurea kai whiria!

Ignore the small issues, address the priorities.

Perspective is everything.

I want to use both of Hina's names for today. Mauri and Maurea. They are both so potent and rich with insight for use as our whakawātea, our clearing, is close to the end. This is the penultimate of Hina's faces for the month.

I am that kid who annoyingly asked why. All the time, and I still do. This is part of who I am, innately curious. So it has been natural for me to ponder and research why our tūpuna, our ancestors in Te Hiku o Te Ika, the Far North, named this moon Maurea. In some places Hina is also known by the name Mauri today. Both of these words speak to our concept of life's essence, life's priorities in their own special ways. Today is the old people's reminder. In this special moment as the light door is closing, we are instructed to explore the meanings of maurea and mauri.

'Tihei mauri ora!'

You may have heard this on the marae, at a work meeting, an event, or on social media perhaps. Literally 'the sneeze of life'. A commonly used saying. This is a way of signalling that the person is about to share their thoughts. The pronouncement itself harks back to when our first human, a woman, Hineahuone, came to life. Hineahuone, the woman fashioned from the earth. Tāne, one of our deities, breathed life into her and she sneezed.

Hina's Mauri face asks, how can we begin to understand our own mauri?

Our esteemed tohunga from Ngāi Tūhoe, Dr Rangimārie Rose Pere, has told us it is the life principle. The source of vitality. Everything has it. Rocks have mauri. Birds, insects, fish have mauri. Seaweed and grass have mauri. Water has mauri. It is the unique life force that enables everything to be alive. Dr Rose also likened mauri to the Greek goddess Psyche. Others have described mauri as the energy that binds the heart and soul together. It is said that our ancestors believed that when we die, the mauri uncouples the body and spirit connection at the ārai. The ārai is the veil, where we cross over into the afterlife in our travels to Hawaiki. These are the lands of Te Hiku that I hail from.

Mauri is what makes us present. We turn up in the world with mauri.

'Ko te mauri he mea huna ki te moana.' Mauri is hidden in the ocean.

'Ko te mauri he mea huna ki te ngāherehere.' Mauri is hidden in the forest.

These two whakatauākī, exquisite proverbial sayings of old, speak volumes about mauri.

The first is attributed to Nukutawhiti, a great voyager from the North. The second is documented in a collection of mōteatea, chants and laments, published in 1853, but dating back much much further.

These whakatauākī invite us to use our wawata,

our dreams, to swim in the ocean teeming with life. To delve into the humming forest. We feel so alive. Just as the whakatauākī indicate. And we sense, all around us, and within us, growth. Have you been into the depths of forests, and on pausing you feel that vibration — plants, trees, birds bursting with life? Swimming in the sea, the waves tickling every pore. The silkiness of sand. The sensuality of life is there and we are part of it. The canopy of trees swaying overhead, the rhythm of the cajoling waves. The beauty of living is that we simply bring whoever we are in that very moment, into these experiences. Connecting with priorities, the essentials of who we are, these open up the way, free of judgement.

These succinct proverbial words of wisdom speak to our life's journey to discover this mauri within us. Our quest, let's say. If something is hidden, the invitation is to find it. Especially if it is hidden right in front of our noses. A kind of ancient hide and seek. How do we enter that discovery? For me, our tūpuna, our forebears, named this face of Hina as a pointed reminder. The way is open for our mauri to flow. For us to discover more about our life's essence. Whether you call this Maurea or Mauri, today Hina invites us into these wawata. Our priorities, our essence.

According to our Okoro, our lunar calendar, Maurea is propitious for planting and spearfishing. Growth and harvest from land and sea. More indicators of the abundance of mauri.

The secrets of both Maurea and Mauri are available, especially today. I am not saying this is easy. There are times when being alive and all of life's mess, all its stress, uncertainty and fear can feel paralysing, even crushing. Those moments of absolute devastation, a numb narrowing of view, when that mauri and those priorities seem to drain away, slipping through our fingers.

Clawing back some sense of our own mauri is today's job. Maybe it feels like the back-breaking work of planting in the māra, the garden. Or, it is as if we are out spearfishing, and miss the proverbial fish and stab ourselves in the foot with the sharp point of the spear on our first few attempts.

Remember, Hina's door stays open tonight. Open to our unique immersion in the light of our floating Maurea moon.

The big question, then, isn't about the overall maurea or mauri of life. The question Hina begs of us, is simply, what is the mauri of *your* life? What are your maurea? What new perspectives can you discover hidden in your wawata today?

Mutuwhenua

Completion

Ko Mutuwhenua tēnei, ko te mihi whakamutunga.

Mutuwhenua, the final tribute, the homecoming.

Relish a moment of completion.

Mutuwhenua is our final homage in this whakawātea, this clearing and closing. Our last wave of the hand before we return to Whiro.

Hina reminds us that this is our omega. Our last salute. Our doffing the cap as we leave the stage. Ready for our next rotation.

There are certain experiences in life that are absolutely clear in showing the connections with our ancestors. In holding us to our path. They remind us to stand strong, no matter how much we are judged. Too enthusiastic, or too humble, or too shy. Too Māori or not Māori enough. Too much or too little of anything. When we realise we can never get it right as far as some others are concerned, no matter how hard we might try. This is our end point. We stand at the end of our journey. Being, and being here now is our unique contribution.

This is where we draw the line. This is Mutuwhenua. This is us.

Pineaha Murray, one of our beloved kaumātua, our respected elders, told me that kuaka, godwits, take a stone from the beach at Pārengarenga to find their way home from the other side of the world on their vast migrations. The stone is magnetised so the birds feel that pull, that source, and that's how they can navigate their way home.

Many years ago, he told me to take a stone from the beach and to keep it in my whare, the house I live in. That stone sat on my bookshelf, waiting.

One day, I was going to meet with an esteemed tohunga, a revered cultural expert from another iwi. I felt a sudden compulsion to have the stone with me, to have that intimate piece of home by my side. To keep me grounded. So the stone remained in my bag.

Soon after, a friend who had interviewed me for her research about Māori Jewish whānau suggested we visit our tupuna, our ancestor, Samuel Yates' grave in the Jewish cemetery in Karangahape Road in Tāmaki Makaurau, Auckland. I had wanted to visit him there for so long and now I would get the chance. I was so excited. We met up at the gated area and she explained some Jewish tikanga, some protocols. All new to me. She pointed out that there were no flowers in the graveyard. This is the Jewish way. Rather than flowers, she told me that their practice is to bring a small stone to place by the graves of their loved ones.

I felt every hair on my body stand up. I could suddenly feel the stone in my bag as if it was a hot coal. Tears welled up. She led me over to Samuel's grave. I stood there and touched the gravestone. I read the inscription: 'Samuel Yates, Pārengarenga, North Cape'.

So the stones from Pārengarenga, they bring us home too. Just like our beloved kuaka.

Standing in that cemetery brings me full circle. A moment where my experience of wairua, of spirit, connecting me back in time with our tūpuna, was so vibrant and real.

Mutuwhenua is the moon to home our focus in on wairua. Wairua has a deeply personal meaning for each of us. And yet we also share some common experiences that indicate how wairua works as another sense. An eye of a different kind. A knowing, an intuition, a tuning in, a vibration. In my work as a psychiatrist I describe wairua as the unique connection between Māori and all aspects of the universe.

When there is disruption to wairua, such as has occurred through colonisation, through displacement, death, suffering, trauma, lack of connection with our lands and language, we see the intergenerational effects. We see the distortions. We feel the mental anguish and pain in a domain beyond the solely psychological. We try what we can to mend that wairua suffering, that cultural injury.

Mutuwhenua invites our healing wawata. Using karakia, prayer, closeness with kaumātua, with our old people, being together on our marae, our tribal gathering spaces, going to the places our ancestors walked, loved, fought and collected kai. Eating kai from home.

Sharing these wairua enhancing experiences.

These activites are the metaphorical stone in the gullet of the kuaka. Wairua is our magnetic force. Our cultural gravity. Strengthing our wairua brings us closer and closer to home, in ourselves and as a group. As whānau. And we need to continue to heal so our generations to come are free of those cultural injuries. Mutuwhenua is Hina's conclusion. Her filigree coronet a final signal, so we can see the lights of home.

Mutuwhenua is a time to renew our commitments to our tūpuna. After all, we are their representatives alive now. Mutu is a word that encompasses many shades of endings. Signalling a time of completion. An extreme stop, so pause here, put the brake on. And let's be ready to go around our lunar cycle again. Ready for another month of wawata, of moon dreaming with Hina.

Index

Āhuatanga hoahoa
A note on design

The design work featured in *Wawata* is inspired by the takarangi spiral. In particular, this intersecting double spiral is defined by the distinct negative and positive spaces that depict the separation of Ranginui and Papatūānuku, implicitly acknowledging humanity's celestial origins.

The takarangi spiral is expressed through whakairo, the traditional Māori practice of subtractive wood carving. Both striking in design and deep in meaning, whakairo patterns are used to adorn objects and taonga whose function facilitates the connection between the mundane and the divine, between Te Pō and Te Ao Mārama. The threshold between these realms, and the potential that lies between them, is in a constant state of flux and is ultimately influenced by the cycles of Hina.

A selection of these taonga is presented in the chapter openers — their daily functions corresponding to the phase of Hina presented in each section. The main image is featured on the left, while the background features the intricacies of the details in varying opacities, layered to reflect the shadows cast in Hina's light. The focus on curvilinear designs exemplifies the female element within these pages, with each chapter's design work summarised as follows:

Kupu arataki, introduction: Tauihu – prow of a waka, traditionally viewed as an omen or new beginning.

Whakaeke: Tiki – symbolises the entrance of humans into Te Ao Mārama at Kurawaka.

Mōteatea: Taiaha – provision to whakawātea, clear negative energies.

Waiata ā-ringa: Pare – reserved for female element to negate wairua when entering a wharenui.

Poi: Waka huia – revelation of contents, preparation and re-assessment of taonga.

Haka: Hoe – channelling energies through the body and mind to move forward.

Whakawātea: Taurapa — stern, or the end of the waka, characterised by prolific takarangi designs.

Luther Ashford
Ngā Rauru Kiitahi, Ngāti Ruanui, Te Pakakohi

He rauemi tāpiri Further resources

Living by the Stars with Professor Rangi Matamua: https://livingbythestars.co.nz/ www.facebook.com/Livingbythestars/

Tuhi Stationery: https://tuhi.co.nz/

Heeni Hoterene: https://manawhenua.com/ www.facebook.com/maramataka/

Riki Solomon & Maria Peach, 'Ngā kitenga o te Maramataka: The insights into the Māori Lunar calendars,' *International Journal of Integrated Care* (2021), vol. 20, no. 1, p. 211. DOI: doi.org/10.5334/ijic.s4211

Lana Andelane, 'The Hui: Maramataka, Matariki and the revival of Māori sciences', *Newshub*, 12 July 2020, https://www.newshub.co.nz/home/new-zealand/2020/07/the-hui-maramataka-matariki-and-the-revival-of-m-ori-sciences.html

He mihi whakakapi Acknowledgements

He waka kōtuia kāhore e tukutukua ngā mimira.

The waka must be securely bound together to prevent it from coming apart.

This book is a waka, with many people contributing to the vessel's integrity on our book's journey. He Waka Kōtuia is also the name of an incredible rangatahi kapa.

This whakataukī feels like a fitting way to express the gratitude for all the support I have felt in bringing this book to life.

Our whaea are a constant source of inspiration. They continue to shine their life lessons onto these pages. Kahurangi Rangimārie Naida Glavish, Whaea Moe Milne, Aunty Mabel Wharekawa-Burt, Whaea Rahera Shortland, Phyllis Tangitu, Te Kaanga Skipper and Professor Khyla Russell, mā, have all been urging me onward in their own magnificent ways.

He puna aroha tō te tamaiti. Millie and Reuben. Being your mum opens up the world in new ways every single day. Poho kererū ana au ki a kōrua.

E te Māmā, ahakoa kua ngaro i te tirohanga kanohi, e kore rawa e ngaro i te pūmahara. Dad, despite your fragile health, you have never stopped encouraging me.

E taku koroua, e Huatahi, e taku toka tū moana, ngā tai o Mihi ka rere ki a koe, e te tau.

Margaret Sinclair, I will always cherish the unconstrained energy and care you have brought to the journey of this book's evolution. Ngā mihi matihere.

E te pononga o Hineteiwaiwa, e taku tuhi mareikura, e te mokopuna o Ngāti Rārua, o Te Ātiawa, o Ngāi Tūhoe. E Nuki, kāore e ārikarika aku mihi ki a koe.

E te iho pūmanawa, Luther, mōu i whakamahiti korou te mahi toi i ēnei wawata, hei whakarāwai, hei whakarētō ēnei whārangi.

Ki a koutou, e te ope kaikākāriki, kei te mōhio pū

koutou, ko wai a koutou. E kore e ea te kupu mihi o te ngākau.

E tōku kaihana piripono, e Peter-Lucas Jones, te kaitiaki o te Okoro, mōu i whakatūwhera ōku karu ki te whakaaro o te ūkaipō, hei ō ake mā tama ā-roto mā hine ā-roto. E te whanaunga, Ted Jones, e tika ana te kōrero, he kanohi kitea ka hoki ngā mahara. Tēnei au e mihi ana!

E te ringa rehe nō Apanui-ringa-mutu, Erica, anei tāku kōrero whakamihi nui. He waewae kai pakiaka koe!

Ki a koutou katoa, e ngā kaipānui nōki, ka mutu, ngā kaihoe o tō Hina waka, tēnei te mihi atu ki a tātou e hīrau ngātahi ana ki tēnei rerenga porotaitaka, ki tēnei rerenga whai hua mō te ao hurihuri nei.

Through 52 whakataukī — traditional Māori life lessons — esteemed psychiatrist Dr Hinemoa Elder shares the power of aroha and explores how it could help all of us every day.

About the author

Dr Hinemoa Elder is of Ngāti Kurī, Te Rarawa, Te Aupōuri and Ngāpuhi descent and is the mother of two adult children.

She has lived on Te Motu Ārai Roa, Waiheke Island for more than 20 years. She is a child and adolescent psychiatrist who works at Starship Hospital's Child & Family and Mother & Baby Units and at various community clinics. Hinemoa also provides youth forensic court reports and neuropsychiatric assessment and treatment of traumatic brain injury in private practice. She is a deputy psychiatry member of the New Zealand Mental Health Review Tribunal.

In 2019, Hinemoa was appointed a Member of the New Zealand Order of Merit for services to psychiatry and Māori. You can also find her on Instagram and Tiktok @drhinemoa.

PENGUIN

UK | USA | Canada | Ireland | Australia
India | New Zealand | South Africa | China

Penguin is an imprint of the Penguin Random House group of companies, whose addresses can be found at global.penguinrandomhouse.com.

First published by Penguin Random House New Zealand, 2022

3 5 7 9 10 8 6 4 2

Design by Cat Taylor © Penguin Random House New Zealand
Cover and endpaper night sky photographs © Mark Gee, cover art © Luther Ashford
Okoro on page 28 and endpapers photographed by Erica Sinclair
Prepress by Soar Communications Group
Printed and bound in China by RR Donnelley

A catalogue record for this book is available from the National Library of New Zealand.

ISBN 978-0-14-377759-5
ISBN 978-0-14-377774-8 (audio)
eISBN 978-0-14-377760-1

penguin.co.nz

Good for water-melons

Good for line & Spearfishing.

Line & Spearfishing.

Water-melons.

Netting.

Best of days for Harpoon, Line & Spearfishing.

SEED BEDS.

Deep Sea Net, Spear. Whitebait fishing. Good for Planting Corn.

Schnapper. Fishing.

Eels, Trout.

BARREN

Good for Kumaras Not large but plentiful.

Some fish caught

Good for crops below ground leve Kumaras, etc.

MUTU
WHENUA
MAUREA
ORONGO
OTANE
TANGAROA ATA
KIOKIO
TANGAROA AROTO
TANGAROA AMUA
KOREKORE PIRI KI TANGAROA
KOREKORE TUARUA
KOREKORE
OIKE
TAKIRAU
RAKAU
MATOHI

30
29
28
27
26
25
24
23
22
21
20
19
18

E